Vegetarian Nights

FRESH FROM HAWAII

BONNIE MANDOE

CELESTIAL ARTS
BERKELEY, CALIFORNIA

Celestial Arts
P.O. Box 7123
Berkeley, California 94707

Cover and text design by Fifth Street Design
Illustrations by Diana Dorenzo

Library of Congress Cataloging-in-Publication Data
Mandoe, Bonnie
    Vegetarian nights : fresh from hawaii / by Bonnie Mandoe
        p.   cm.
    Includes index.
    ISBN 0-89087-712-2
    1. Vegetarian cookery. 2. Cookery — Hawaii. I. Title.
TX837.M288   1994
641.5'636 — dc20   93-49055
                                                       CIP

Printed in the United States of America

First Printing 1994
1 2 3 4 5 / 98 97 96 95 94

The silver rain, the shining sun
The fields where scarlet poppies run
And all the ripples of the wheat
Are in the bread that I do eat.

So when I sit for every meal
And say a grace, I always feel
That I am eating rain and sun
And fields where scarlet poppies run.

– Anonymous

This book is dedicated
to my husband Niels,
whose company, humor, and good hard work
continue to inspire me,
year after year.

Acknowledgments

Writing this book has been a pleasure. Both the time in the kitchen and the time at the computer have been free times — hours of joyous, creative release. As I look back on the process, there are many people I want to thank. I've been taught, supported, encouraged, and otherwise moved to action by so many — from children to chiropractors; from philosopers to farmers. And by the musicians, poets, and artists of the ages. By ordinary people, and by Mother Nature herself.

"Aloha" to one and all. It means everything from "Greetings" to "Farewell," and it also means to venerate and to remember with affection. Aloha, my friends, beginning with this list, and ending with you, dear reader, as my gratitude is passed along here.

Aloha and mahalo to Anne and Bill Caminker, my parents, for unconditional love and support; to Robin Lim, for setting off the spark that sent me to Celestial Arts; to Mollie Katzen, for exemplary generosity of spirit and for walking me through; to Dave Hinds, my publisher, for Seeing the Bigger Picture and for laughing a lot; to Jackie Wan, who — in less than a sentence — gave me the best constructive criticism I've ever had; to copyeditor Colleen Paretty for clarity of thought; to Fifth Street Design for these beautiful pages; to Diana Dorenzo, not only for the artwork I love, but for inspiring the artist in me, too; and to Veronica Randall, managing editor, who kept it all moving; to my friends and family whose images appear in the artwork; to Lynne Horner and David Hoff at The Maui News, for trust at the beginning and good humor throughout our twelve years together; to Michael Kanouff, Duane Garrett, my son Bo Mandoe, and Steve Slater, for computer wizardry and patience extraordinare; to my daughter, Prana Mandoe, for the unspoken and for loving the leftovers; to Katrina Buchanan, my right hand in the kitchen and talented chef in her own right; to Summer Richardson, for Being There, always; to my friend and favorite Clean Person, Tim Tremaine; to my much-appreciated chiropractors, Gary Ryan and Russ Rosen; to my long-term clients and fellow tantrikas, Charles and Caroline Muir; to Dr. Elaine Willis, for inspiration; to the stores and wholesalers who provide the raw materials for it all: Down To Earth, Mana Foods, Fred's Maui, Hamasaki's, Maui Style, Tri-O Farms, and Teruya Tofu Factory; and to those people I've met through books and music, who have added immeasurably to my life: Johnny Clegg, Paul Simon, and The Grateful Dead; to Hazrat Inayat Khan, H.L. Poonja, Chogyam Trungpa, and Deepak Chopra, for saying what can't be said. My heartfelt aloha; I love you all.

Table of Contents

Why Vegetarian Nights?

Fifteen years ago I took a job, having no idea of the effect it would have on my life: I agreed to prepare food for a seminar. Until then, I'd been content to cook for my family and friends, but that first catering job was so satisfying, it evolved into an ongoing business — Maui's first vegetarian catering company.

I kept a file of recipes and tended it like a garden, regularly adding the compost and pulling the weeds of my experience. As the file grew, entire menus emerged in the place of isolated recipes. The most satisfying comment the food evoked (and still evokes) is, "If I could just cook and eat like this every day, it would be easy to change to a lighter, less meat-oriented diet." Although I hear it all the time, the words always lift my spirits; I know we can eat like this every day.

I also know how difficult it is to change our diets. It's a formidable task to break any habit, and the roots of our food choices go deep. A new balance must be established, and this requires patience.

In the course of time, my collection changed. Fewer egg- and cheese-rich dishes were called for, and more Asian foods, stir-fries, and roasted specialties found their way onto the menu. But my love of the work has never changed — from harvesting our own fruits and vegetables, to introducing people to a new way of eating. I delight in their amazement at finding that something good for them also tastes good. For my part, I enjoy eating what I cook and watching my weight remain stable. And I continue to have a great time combining colors, tastes, and textures, turning ordinary ingredients into extraordinary food.

Obviously, I can't cook for everyone. But through this book, I can share the pleasures of our table with those of you I haven't met. And I can, at last, present this collection to those of you who've been waiting for it. You'll find the recipes that generated the greatest enthusiasm over the years and also new ones only the taste-testers have tried.

The message in these pages is simple. Despite the overall challenge of changing our diets, it's surprisingly easy to make fabulous food without meat. Most of the groups I cook for are not vegetarians; they're people who discover that anyone can savor a vegetarian night. Or create one of their own. It just takes willingness, the right ingredients, and some recipes that really work.

Part One:

Considerations, Suggestions, Inspirations

Gathering the Ingredients

Collecting ingredients is the first step when putting a dish together. It's a step I used to omit, preferring to "get started." Now, I use the time I'm collecting ingredients to collect myself, too.

It's practical to have everything you need on the counter before you begin cooking. If something's missing, you'll notice right away. Gathering also allows time to take your culinary pulse. Do you really feel like making this dish?

It's good for me, and for the food I'm cooking, to have a certain enthusiasm for the project, even if it's something I've made before. If the enthusiasm isn't there, why bother?

From my perspective, cooking food isn't some dull chore that's fallen in my lap. It's part of a much larger picture. It's one of the ways I relate to myself, my family, and the world. It's part of a choice I make every day about the way I take care of things. No one forces me to eat what I eat, or cook what I cook. The choice is mine. Every time I set ingredients on the counter to prepare a dish, I make that choice again.

Variables

It may seem mysterious that the same recipe, prepared by three individuals, comes out tasting three different ways. But that's the nature of individuals, and we've all experienced it. My goal is to make the instructions for recipes in this book so clear that every version satisfies. With this in mind, the following are some factors often responsible for major differences in cooking results.

Oven Temperature

Never assume that your oven bakes at the temperature set on the dial. Purchase an oven thermometer (they're available in some supermarkets, and certainly in kitchen shops) and test it. A difference of 25 degrees — a significant difference — is common.

Measuring Technique

Do you measure dry ingredients accurately, leveling off the measuring cup with the back of a knife, or do you prefer to "eyeball it," as I often do? There's nothing wrong with using your inborn measuring skills, if they're sharp, and if you don't mind some variation in results. Accurate measurement is most crucial when baking cakes, so take special care, especially the first time you use a recipe.

Pan Size and Type

Selecting the proper pan for baking a cake or quick bread is essential to a recipe's success. Still, this crucial detail is often overlooked, even in many otherwise good cookbooks.

A pan's size is significant because of the effect it has on baking time. For example, a cake baked in an 8-inch square pan has a surface area of 64 square inches. If it were baked instead in a 7 by ll-inch pan, the cake would have 77 square inches of surface area. It would be thinner and it would dry out or burn if baked the length of time given for the 8 by 8-inch pan.

Similarly, a quick bread designed to fill a 9 by 5-inch pan would be thicker if it were baked in an 8 by 4½-inch pan; it would need more time to bake.

A pan's material is also important. I prefer baking in shiny stainless steel because the shine reflects heat from the sides of the pan, keeping the edges of cakes and cookies from becoming dark and overdone. Black pans, on the other hand, attract heat and are perfect for baking crusty breads. Glass pans transmit heat quickly; if you use them, reduce the oven temperature by 25 degrees.

Chopping Style

Vegetable chopping is a practical art. You may or may not appreciate the art; you may or may not enjoy chopping vegetables. But in either case, you do want to keep your fingers out of the way. To do so, lay the vegetable on a long, cut edge you have made with your knife. This gives you a solid foundation. It's difficult to cut a rocking carrot or a rolling parsnip. Also, keep the fingers of your non-cutting hand tucked under (in typing position), rather than fully extended.

That said, let me also mention that there is no "right" way to chop vegetables. The right way is the way you like them. But consider this: A woman who worked for me had previously owned her own restaurant and had managed its staff of forty. She was skilled, capable, and successful. She once made a mushroom sauce for twenty-five people from my recipe. I like mushrooms in thick, meaty chunks; she minced them. That one difference changed the character of the sauce completely, to say the least. If you want to experience the recipes in this book as they were intended to be made, follow the chopping instructions carefully.

There are six basic cuts used in this book, and three differ only according to size.

To **dice** means to chop in pieces roughly ⅜- to ½-inch square.

To **mince** means to chop much more finely — as finely as you can, in fact.

Larger chunks, up to 1-inch square, are called **bite-sized.**

A **roll cut** is used to make chunks, large or small, from long cylindrical vegetables like carrots and zucchini. It's a rather time-consuming process, as the vegetable is turned (about a quarter turn) after every diagonal cut. The benefit of this cut is that every chunk of vegetable contains a portion of center as well as a portion of skin.

A **half moon** is a cut applied only to onions, and it produces attractive shapes more accurately described as crescents. Cut a peeled onion in two from stem to stem, then lay the vegetable on the cut surfaces. Cut slices, again from stem to stem. The distance between your slices will determine the thickness of your crescents.

A **julienne** indicates long, thin, even slivers, like matchsticks. The pieces may be shorter or thicker than matchsticks; it is their uniformity that makes them stand out in a dish. Cutting coarse vegetables such as carrots in a fine julienne, makes them cook very quickly.

Weather

Humidity, temperature, and barometric pressure influence us, as well as the food we cook. Paying attention to these conditions stimulates us to cook appropriately. We do this in part by instinct — when it's hot, we crave cool foods; when it's cold, we crave warmth. When it's humid (moisture in the air), we crave moisture in our bodies. When the barometer (and our energy level) drops, our appetites diminish too. Simple attention to weather can stimulate creativity in the kitchen.

Mood

Naturally, what is cooked is colored by the cook. Too obvious to mention — but too important to omit. One school of thought about nutrition tells us not to eat when we're emotionally out of balance; that ordinary foods become toxic when our body chemistry is affected by anger, sorrow, or even intense excitement.

It's the same with cooking. The mood of the chef is expressed in every vegetable she chops, in every sandwich she assembles, in every crust she throws away. For this reason, we feel it when food is prepared with love and attention, and we feel it when food is thrown together in anger or despair.

If it sounds like there's a message here, for me it's this: I cook when I feel like cooking. Otherwise, I like to keep our meals very simple.

Playing with Fire

When we cook, we put the power of fire to work. It's easier for us to turn on a burner than it was for our foremothers to stoke up a woodburning stove, but the result is the same. The element of fire, located at the center of the earth and again at the center of our solar system, is likewise alive and cooking in the center of our kitchens. For myself, I find what must be a primitive satisfaction in utilizing this potent force of nature.

In every action, there is an opportunity, and where but in the act of cooking do we have the daily opportunity to work with fire? Maybe that's why I've never minded standing over the stove . . . and why I'm not attracted to microwave ovens at all.

Our kitchen fires (the appliances that sustain home cooking) produce two types of heat — dry and moist. The better we understand the workings of each, the better they can serve us.

Dry Heat

Broiling, baking, roasting, and sautéing are the dry-heat techniques used in this book. The first three are similar in that they all happen in the oven — where small differences of technique make rather large differences in your results. Sautéing is a dry process because heat is transferred to the food through its contact with fat, rather than water.

In **broiling,** high heat is used from above only. It is an interesting method for quick-cooking vegetables such as tomatoes, mushrooms, and peppers, and is also excellent for top-browning, when a crust is desired, as in cheese-topped or potato casseroles. In many home ovens, there is only one temperature offered for broiling, and it is the maximum heat. To prevent scorching, food may be lowered from the fire.

Baking, the most common method of oven cooking, is the simple process of placing foods, uncovered, in a preheated oven and leaving them there until done. Remember to place the oven rack or racks where you want them before the oven is heated. It's best to use one rack only, if possible, because in baking, the more the air circulates, the better. Crowding the oven lengthens baking time and invites uneven distribution of heat. If two racks must be used, stagger the pans so they don't block heat from each other, and rotate them once during baking.

For optimal results, position baked goods appropriately in the oven. Cakes, cookies, and breads are happiest just above center, where the tops take advantage of the rising heat and brown nicely, and the bottoms aren't dangerously close to the fire. Items that rise significantly, like soufflés, should be placed slightly below the oven's center, allowing for maximum expansion and easy removal from the oven.

Roasting is much like baking but, for vegetarian purposes, it is done at much higher heat. In the 450- to 500- degree F. range, roasting brings out the best in a vegetable's flavor by searing the outside, thus holding in the juices, and cooking the inside in one quick blaze. Vegetables should be tossed in a bit of oil first, then roasted eight to twelve minutes. Sprinkle with salt, pepper, and/or herbs when the veggies come out of the oven.

Sautéing, to be authentic, is a rather exacting technique in which hot oil, high heat, and totally dry food combine to produce a dish whose own moisture is held wholly intact. Nothing moist is added to the pan; that would cause steam, which destroys the sauté effect. Sautéing is the same as shallow-fat frying.

Moist Heat

The varied moist-heat processes I use include boiling, simmering, braising, steaming, casseroling, and pressure cooking. Each term refers to a specific combination of heat and moisture, as follows.

Boiling is an intense application of heat to liquid, causing raucous bubbling when the water reaches 212 degrees F. In most cases, this technique is too violent to benefit the food; beans, for example, fall apart when boiled. But boiling is definitely the best technique to use for readying a pot of water for pasta. Before the pasta is added, keep the pot covered to retain the heat; once the pasta is added, uncover and reduce the heat, if necessary, to produce a slower boil. Even pasta breaks apart when boiled too hard.

Simmering is a common stove-top process which involves low heat. Simmering brings a soup, stew, or bean pot to 135 to 185 degrees F. and produces slight bubbling. This gentle process protects fragile foods and tenderizes them at the same time.

Braising is a stove-top cooking method in which foods are first lightly fried, uncovered, in a small amount of hot oil (or even water), then completed with liquid. This is my stove-top cooking method of choice because it uses the least fat. Cooking in a wok is a perfect example. First, vegetables are cooked in a bit of oil (or water) over high heat, then the heat is reduced and soy sauce, or a mixed sauce, is added. When I cook with this method using no fat, I usually add a teaspoon or two of a flavored oil after the dish has been cooked. This adds richness to the finished dish without heating the oil.

Steaming is a simple and popular way to prepare vegetables. The vegetables are cooked in a perforated basket above — not in — simmering water, thus retaining all the nutrients. When steaming, remember to reduce the heat to a simmer after the water boils. This helps cook the vegetables gently and evenly. If more than one type of vegetable is to be steamed, start the vegetable that requires the most time (such as beets) first. Add quick-cooking vegetables such as snap peas at the very end. And if you have time, make a sauce. Steamed vegetables are delicious with even the simplest of sauces.

Casseroling is simply baking food with a cover. In the process, the oven's heat is captured in the casserole, creating steam, and the steam bastes the dish as it cooks.

Pressure cooking is a quick and efficient method that works wonders on dried beans. It also saves time in cooking coarse vegetables like sweet potatoes and artichokes. Follow the directions that came with the cooker you own. The major danger with pressure cooking is overcooking, so be careful.

Chef's Tools

Nonelectric Tools

Like other artists, we kitchen artists have our essential tools. Certain ones — my ginger grater, for example — feel almost like part of the family. My husband Niels, found it in the dirt under a house we rented behind Piiholo Hill in 1978. I have no idea where it came from originally; the handle is made of horn, and the holes are tiny and sharp-edged. It grates ginger, garlic, and citrus peel more finely than any tool I've encountered.

There is particular satisfaction in having the right tool for a specific job, and the more you cook, the more you appreciate the tool that makes it easy. My **spoon-shaped rubber spatula** has come to seem like an extension of my own hands. This is the tool for scraping every last bit of cake batter from the mixing bowl and every lick of honey from the measuring cup. (I've heard it called a "child-cheater.") I have several of them in the utensil crock, so there's always one at hand. The spoon shape is a definite improvement on the flat shape; my flat scrapers are long gone.

Plastic strainers are high on my list of favorite tools because they're easy to clean (whack them on the bottom of the sink), and they don't corrode like metal ones do. They are inordinately strong. We have a graduated set, one of which is usually in the drying rack, having just performed some notable function — sifted the lumps out of baking soda, strained the seeds from a lemon, or held beans as I rinsed them under the tap.

It has taken years for me to weed the poor quality utensils from my collection and gather stauncher varieties. I've replaced our garlic press, the potato masher, and the wire whisk, to name a few. The process has been enjoyable because each upgrade has been the result of discovering something better.

I've learned that cheap kitchen tools are never a bargain. If you buy quality tools the first time, you can use them for a lifetime.

The only immediate purchase you might want to make would be to replace any aluminum pots and pans that live in your kitchen. Since aluminum is porous, it absorbs food particles into its microscopic "pores." When these particles eventually rot and dislodge, they could deposit aluminum they've leached from the pot right into your dinner. Aluminum poisioning is dangerous and has been associated with Alzheimer's disease.

Cast iron is my material of choice for sauté pans. I like the heaviness of cast iron, and the way it distributes heat evenly. I can't remember ever burning anything in cast iron. The combination of heat and oil builds a protective coating on the pan with use, and eventually this coating works much like that of a non-stick pan. But cast iron doesn't take kindly to water or acidic foods like vinegar and tomatoes; these substances disintegrate the protective coating and eventually cause rust. To preserve my cast-iron pans, I use stainless steel for sautéing with water and for cooking acidic items.

Most of my pots and pans are made of **stainless steel.** Like glass, stainless has a clean feel. It doesn't absorb odors or particles of food, and heavy-duty stainless cookware conducts heat well. It's perfect for cooking rice. My favorite stainless pots have extra-heavy bottoms (usually aluminum clad in stainless) to provide better heat distribution and protection against scorching. Lightweight stainless is good for boiling pasta water quickly.

Nonstick skillets are immensely valuable if they're of the highest quality — that is, guaranteed scratch-proof. It's a pleasure to use these high-tech tools that reduce our dependence on oils and fats for cooking. But inexpensive nonstick skillets are a waste of money. Their surfaces are easily scratched, exposing the underlying aluminum and making the pan virtually useless. No one wants them, so they end up at the thrift shop or the dump; they shouldn't be produced in the first place.

No tribute to kitchen tools would be complete without a word about **knives.** A high-quality, well-weighted, sharp kitchen knife brings joy to the hand and heart of any chef. Even a novice can appreciate the comfort and precision of a well-designed knife. It sits in the hand without tension, and the blade glides through the skin, flesh, and seeds of

Other tools that make my kitchen an amusing, as well as a practical place, include:

- strong wooden spoons for mixing
- 1-quart glass measuring cup (for liquid measure)
- graduated stainless steel measuring cups (for dry measure)*
- graduated stainless steel measuring spoons*
- large colander
- stainless steel baking pans in a variety of sizes
- stainless steel cookie sheets
- graduated mixing bowls
- wire rack for cooling baked goods
- vegetable peeler
- wire whisk
- narrow & wide spatulas
- potato masher
- eggbeater
- rolling pin
- grater
- ladle
- salad spinner
- pastry brush
- pastry blender
- tongs
- stainless steel garlic press
- stainless steel ice-cream scoop

Stainless steel measuring utensils come in various qualities.

Notes from my Maui kitchen . . .

The kitchen is right in the middle of our house. It's a big, light room with yellow walls and sky-blue counters. The floor is made of smooth-as-silk oak boards that my husband installed, sanded, and finished himself.

all fruits and vegetables with ease. Without a good knife, a watermelon is hard to handle; a big pumpkin can be downright dangerous.

It's amazing how many American homes function without the benefit of a good knife — and how many men and women don't even realize the lack. It's like the difference between a toy and a tool. In the average kitchen, it would take only one good chopping knife (a wedge-shaped blade six to eight inches long that runs the full length of the handle), and a small paring knife of equal quality, to make a dramatic change. With a good knife, chopping vegetables is a pleasure, not a chore.

For your knives, you'll eventually need a sharpening rod and some hands-on sharpening guidance from a friend or teacher. You'll also want a large chopping board, preferably of wood.

If you want the best tools, you may have to order them by mail or search them out in a better-than-average kitchen store. The handles of first-quality measuring tools don't bend or fall off, and the measurement amounts are precise. It's worth the cost and effort to obtain them.

Electric Tools

The **blender** is by far the most used electric tool in my kitchen. It works foods to the smoothest possible consistency, and for this I forgive the noise it makes, which is considerable. I approach the blender like I do the ocean — with respect. It has no built-in safety feature like a food-processor does; you're supposed to be smart enough to keep your fingers and utensils out of the blades. I've lost the tip of a few rubber spatulas and even chipped a wooden spoon or two. It's a serious tool, and it does an outstanding job making creamy soups without cream, as well as dips, sauces, smoothies, frostings, milkshakes, and pie fillings.

The **food processor** is a new addition to my home kitchen and I can still take it or leave it. For catering, it's a valuable time-saver, particularly for grating carrots, shredding cabbage, and chopping parsley. At home, though, for small quantities, it is usually quicker to use a knife.

The **electric mixer** is convenient, but again, I use it more for catering than at home. The fact is, I like using my muscles to beat a cake batter smooth, or to whip cream. I need the exercise.

The **pressure cooker** is one of the most underused, and underappreciated tools in American kitchens. It is truly a time- and energy-saver, especially for vegetarian meals, in which long-cooking foods like barley, rice, and beans are staples. The pressure cooker saves fuel and nutrients, and can reduce cooking time by as much as 75 percent! With pressure, a rich and hearty vegetarian stew can be ready in less than an hour. Making Mexican food from scratch doesn't take all day. And a simple steamed vegetable like cauliflower is done in ten minutes.

Everyone's heard horror stories about the pressure cooker, and it must be fear of an accident that prevents people from taking advantage of this incomparable device. But its design and performance were perfected years ago, and stories of exploding cookers belong to the era of hand-crank cars. There are none left on the road.

If you follow the directions that come with the pot, the biggest danger with the pressure cooker is overcooking your food. It's hard to believe pinto beans could be done in twenty minutes, for example, but that's how long they take. As a rule, pressure cooking takes one third the time of conventional cooking methods.

The most important reason to consider investing in a pressure cooker is this: It gives you the opportunity to serve and eat dried beans more often. Beans are, of course, the seeds of leguminous plants. Even when dried, they can be soaked and sprouted; they are alive. They are notably high in protein, low in fat, and free of cholesterol. In short, they're the perfect protein food for the human body — even the most active and hard-working bodies among us. And with pressure, they're quick to cook.

Tips for use: Follow the safety instructions that come with the cooker or borrow a library book on the subject. Don't attempt to use a pressure cooker without knowing the function of every part. A book or manual will explain the basic procedures, such as never filling the pot more than two thirds of capacity, and not cooking beans such as split peas, which may clog the pressure vent. Keep rubber rings in the cooker lid and around the steam vent absolutely clean. Remain in or near the kitchen when the cooker is in use.

Seasonings

Seeds, leaves, roots, bulbs, bark, buds, and berries — our spice shelves are a mirror of the seasons. Sometimes language gets it totally right — as in "seasonings." These essential plants impart the seasons into our food.

Most herbs and spices retain an acceptable degree of freshness for about a year. After that, they become old and boring. The green leaves go dull, the red peppers go brown, and the rich, earthy hues go gray. Better use none, rather than stale reminders of seasons gone by.

Fresh (and freshly dried) herbs and spices are concentrated substances; using them well is a talent based on experience. Because even small amounts can make a big difference, there's not an enormous margin for error with seasonings. For this reason, many people are timid with them, using only a pinch here and a quarter-teaspoon there. I find these amounts are often indistinguishable, and that it takes more than I would have imagined to make a perceptible statement of flavor. While it's true that subtlety is sometimes appropriate, other times it pays to be daring. Discovering the right spices — and the right amounts — for a particular dish is one of the most exciting aspects of cooking.

There are no hard and fast rules for seasoning, fortunately, and the only standard to meet is one's own sense of what tastes good. So obviously, the following list is one of opinions, not facts, and is meant for purposes of inspiration only.

The Salt Family

The story of salt is a strange one. Its reputation has swung like a pendulum from "essential to good health," to "hazardous to good health," in a few short years.

In fact, both descriptions are true. The issue is quantity. Salt makes up about 0.9 percent of the body's cells and blood; the body must have salt in order to function. Although it is plentiful in nature, both on land and at sea, at one time salt was so scarce and precious that it was used as money. In ancient Rome, soldiers received part of their pay in salt. This was called their salarium, from which the word "salary" is derived. When a person was "not worth their salt," it was meant literally.

Today, salt is inexpensive and widely available. Over 14,000 applications for it have been described (surprisingly, less than 5 percent is used at the table). A great deal of salt is used in food processing, however, especially by meat packers, canned food producers, and manufacturers of dairy products. Overuse of salt has been linked with health problems such as hypertension and heart disease.

Salt is one of the five great tastes, in the auspicious company of the sweet, sour, bitter, and pungent flavors. Of the five, it is the only essential one. The body recognizes this and craves it when it's lacking.

Personal taste for salt varies. For this reason, in the recipes which follow, please take the salt measurement as a suggestion only. Start with a lesser amount and work up to the full amount (or more) to taste.

To my palate, salt is the single most important seasoning, and if overuse is a health hazard — underuse is a taste hazard. For this reason, I use a variety of substances to add that essential salty flavor to foods. Each of the following items adds salt and a splash of its own personality to the foods we love: seasoned salt (such as Spike brand), sesame salt (also called gomasio), miso, soy sauce, and other liquid seasonings such as ume plum vinegar and Bragg's Aminos (a registered trademark).

Green Herbs

Fresh green herbs are a real delight to cook with and to eat. They vary enormously in potency and appropriate usage. In the Savory Vegetables recipe, for example, sprigs of rosemary are roasted with onions, sweet potatoes, beets, and garlic; then the herb is discarded. The rosemary's piney flavor becomes infused in the dish even though it is never eaten. Other fresh herbs (like basil leaves) are so mild they can be torn up like lettuce and tossed into a salad.

The flavor of green herbs changes slightly, and in most cases, becomes more concentrated when the plants are dried. For this reason, I use a smaller quantity of dried herbs than fresh herbs in cooking. In most cases, I prefer whole leaf herbs to powdered herbs. The exception is sage, which is easier to measure and distribute evenly in powdered form.

When using dried herbs, add them during the last half of the cooking process so their flavor remains clear and strong.

Basil is easy to use, rarely overpowers, and is always good with tomatoes, grains, and in salad dressings.

Bay leaf is a subtle taste, good in soups, stews, and curries.

Chinese parsley (also known as **cilantro** and **coriander leaf**) does not dry well; the dried leaf bears no resemblance to the strong, savory taste of the fresh herb. Fresh Chinese parsley is essential to Oriental, Thai, and Mexican cuisines.

Dill weed, both fresh and dried, is the taste we associate with pickles. It's good with potatoes, cucumbers, and in herb bread.

Marjoram is the mild cousin of oregano. Use it in soups, gravies, and herb bread.

Mint is among the freshest of flavors, and is often paired with fruit for this reason. The taste and fragrance of mint is clean and inviting.

Oregano is the pizza herb. It's also good in grain dishes, such as pilaf. Start with a small amount; the flavor is strong.

Parsley is the most popular herb in my kitchen. It dries well, but is usually available fresh year-round. **Curly-leaf parsley** is the most common variety; its fluffy leaves are decorative (but slightly scratchy to the throat when eaten raw). **Flat-leaf (Italian) parsley** is slightly milder in taste and doesn't irritate the throat. Parsley is bitter in flavor, a rather rare quality, which sets it apart from most garden edibles. Bitters have always been prized for their potent medicinal qualities, and parsley is no exception. Add it to cooked dishes at the last minute to make the most of its brilliant color and nutrients.

Rosemary is a strong-flavored, resinous herb. The leaves are stiff and never become soft, so its uses are limited. The flavor is earthy and satisfying.

Sage is the flavor we first tasted (and loved) on Thanksgiving. It is essential to stuffings and mock sausages.

Tarragon has a mild, licorice-like flavor. It's potent, so start with a small amount. It's a good addition to salad dressing.

Thyme is delicious with grains, in soups, and with sweet vegetables like carrots and squash.

Seeds

Seeds are potent little packages of life-to-be. For their size, the amount of flavor they contain is astounding. As good as they are raw, something even more wonderful happens to the taste and texture of seeds when they are lightly roasted. Consider how roasting improves the flavors of sesame, sunflower, and pumpkin seeds, for example.

Anise seed is slightly sweet and licorice-like in flavor.

Caraway seed is delicious in rye bread. It's also good with cabbage, potatoes, and cheese.

Cardamom seeds are an essential ingredient in Danish pastry. If you love Danish, but never knew why, you may have been intoxicated by the pervasive flavor of cardamom. Cardamom seeds are usually purchased in ground form.

Celery seeds are tiny. They're great in potato salad and as a delicate garnish atop savory rolls.

Coriander seed is one of the fundamental ingredients of curry powder. It is also, along with garlic, one of the chief flavorings of the hot dog. The seeds themselves are round and hollow and best used in ground form. The taste of coriander is robust; to my palate, it works better in combinations than on its own.

Cumin seed, both whole and ground, is an important ingredient in chili powder, curry powder, and many ethnic dishes.

Dill seeds have a strong, "green" flavor (stronger than dill weed), and a pleasant, firm texture. They're good with mild vegetables like cucumber, potatoes, and lightly cooked cabbage.

Mustard seeds have a deep, earthy flavor and a multitude of uses. In addition to being the base of one of the world's most popular condiments, they are equally valuable in spice mixtures like curry powder, and in many salad dressings. Whole brown mustard seeds sautéed in oil add a pungent, nutty flavor to curries and other Indian dishes.

Nutmeg has a strong, appealing flavor that works well with sweets and savories alike. A pinch of ground nutmeg (or a grating of the whole kernel), adds a pleasurable, almost mysterious air to dishes that contain spinach, and to rich white sauces.

Poppy seeds are festive, chewy, and slightly sweet. They're particularly appealing in baked goods.

Sesame seeds are tasty, crunchy, and full of calcium. Roasting enhances the flavor significantly. They can be roasted on the stove-top, in a pan without oil over medium heat, until fragrant and lightly browned (about ten minutes). Stir frequently. Or, place them in the oven for about ten minutes at 300 degrees. When they are good and hot, they jump in the pan; that means they're done. Sprinkle toasted sesame seeds atop sweets and savories alike. Store them in the refrigerator or freezer.

Sunflower seeds are a longtime favorite. I remember the first field of sunflowers I saw as my family drove through France. All the big flower heads were turned in the same direction — toward the sun, of course. They looked like spectators at a tennis match. But I loved sunflowers even before that, from the time we had some growing in our yard when I was small. They were giant flowers, taller than my six-foot father, and when the seeds were ready, they fell at our feet.

Roots and Bulbs

The chef's own cache of buried treasures . . .

Ginger is pungent and hot to the taste when eaten alone, but becomes surprisingly tame when sweetened, as in cookies, cakes, and pies. It's a zesty flavor, essential in Oriental dishes that are fresh, light, and sharp.

Turmeric, best known as the spice that gives curry its golden color, is slightly bitter to the taste.

Garlic and **onions** are two essential flavors found in almost every ethnic cuisine. Varieties abound, ranging from huge cloves of elephant garlic (mild in flavor and potato-like in texture), to the delicate, lily-like flowers of wild field garlic (crisp, sweet, and only mildly garlicky in taste). Onions vary enormously too, from eye-stinging to apple-sweet, and from white to burgundy in hue. Try them all.

Bark, Buds, and Berries

These fragrant spices, grown in exotic places, lend intrigue to baked goods.

Cinnamon smells good, wholesome, and safe. Its fragrance works like magic in creating a homey and inviting atmosphere, even when it's just sprinkled lightly on a steamed apple.

Cloves are potent. A pinch is plenty in most recipes; more is overpowering. Sometimes it's fun to add a few whole cloves to a pot of rice just for the mystery of it. Remove them before serving the rice. And see if anyone notices.

Allspice hints at the flavors of cinnamon, nutmeg, and cloves. It is used in pickling.

Spice Combinations

Chili powder is a mixture of a variety of chiles; it may also include garlic, salt, cumin, oregano, coriander, allspice (and anything else the spicemaker is inspired to use). Freshness is crucial with chili powder, as chiles lose their flavor fast and turn musty with age. I use chili powder by the tablespoon rather than the teaspoon; the flavor is not as concentrated as that of curry powder.

Curry powder is a combination of spices. Its characteristic golden color comes from the turmeric root, and its savory flavor from a blend of aromatic spices such as cumin seed, coriander seed, mustard, ginger, cayenne, fenugreek, and cinnamon. Each brand of curry is made from a unique recipe, so no two brands taste exactly alike. Imported Indian brands are most interesting and authentic, but the very best curries are made by grinding and blending your own spices for absolute freshness.

I can't recommend a brand of curry powder because I never buy it; I make my own. If you buy curry powder, purchase small quantities to assure freshness. Try several brands until you find one you're wild about.

Cooking with a Full Tank

The best method I know to stimulate creativity in the kitchen is to keep a well-stocked pantry. Beautiful orange lentils, gnarly dried mushrooms, lacy sheets of purple nori, and myriad other colorful and textural edibles provide inspiration like food itself provides nutrition.

Keeping my pantry full means I rarely buy on impulse. Better yet, I often avoid paying retail. Knowing what I'll need before I need it gives me the opportunity to buy through a neighborhood co-op and to take advantage of supermarket specials. It means that regular shopping trips are brief because they're limited to perishable items like vegetables, bread, fruits, and dairy products.

The chief benefit of a well-stocked pantry is the feeling of satisfaction it brings. I can make a meal that suits the needs of a specific day — its weather, mood, and schedule — without going to the store. That makes me happy. I enjoy staying home when I'm home. In addition, I have the security of knowing there's plenty stored up for a rainy day or a hurricane.

It takes some organization to set up an efficient pantry, but it's the kind of project that can make a real difference in your life. Because our kitchen is a busy, lively place, we rarely eat at restaurants. This "home-centeredness" is not only economical, but is fundamental to our family's togetherness. This year Niels and I celebrate our twenty-second wedding anniversary, so I'm fairly sure it works.

What It Takes

Every person's pantry list will differ according to personal preferences. Here are mine.

Basic dry goods: choice of pastas (I keep wheat and buckwheat on hand); salt, pepper, and a selection of herbs and spices; dried fruits; beans such as lentils, pintos, kidney beans, black-eyed peas, and split peas; thickeners like kuzu, cornstarch, and agar-agar; baking aids like soda and aluminum-free baking powder; vegetable bouillon; and an assortment of sea vegetables like hijiki, wakame, dulse, and kombu.

Basic perishable staples: carrots, onions, potatoes, beets; yeast; butter; honey and maple syrup; nuts and nut butters in season; seeds for eating (sunflower, sesame, and pumpkin) and sprouting (alfalfa); Kalamata olives; whole grains such as brown rice, millet, barley, rye, and popcorn; ground and rolled grains such as oats, cornmeal, whole wheat flour, and rice flour; miso; soymilk; granola or muesli; asceptic-packed tofu; and eggs.

Basic canned and bottled items: a varied selection of oils and vinegars; sherry or mirin (Japanese rice sweetener); Dijon mustard; soy sauce or alternative; vanilla and almond extracts; whole canned tomatoes and/or tomato sauce; tomato paste; water chestnuts; and canned chiles.

Basic frozen items: coconut milk; whole wheat and/or corn tortillas; frozen peas and frozen chopped spinach; tempeh; sometimes phyllo dough.

Preserved Foods . . . without Preservatives

Thinking of natural foods, we think first of fresh foods. But natural foods may also be preserved — without preservatives. Wholesome preserved foods are convenient and can be economical to use, both on a daily basis and when fresh foods aren't available. There are four methods of preserving foods. Chemical preservatives are not essential to any of the four preserving processes, yet they are used frequently nonetheless. To avoid eating preservatives when unnecessary, read package labels.

Dried Foods

When foods are dried naturally, nothing is added and nothing is lost but a percentage of moisture. Fruits and vegetables (which by nature have high water contents) are changed dramatically in the process of drying. Fruits become sweeter when dried. For example, a banana is 85 percent water and 15 percent natural sugar when ripe. Dried, the percentages are reversed. Dried bananas are like candy to eat, as are figs, pineapples, pears, and grapes (raisins).

Be aware that most commercially dried fruits are treated with sulfur dioxide, which preserves their color. The taste of this preservative is particularly obnoxious in dried apricots and golden raisins. Shopping in a reputable health food store makes it easier to find clean, quality dried fruits.

Drying is the most common method of preserving sea vegetables; it is also effective in preserving certain land vegetables and fungi. Tomatoes, onions, and shiitake mushrooms respond particularly well to drying. The water in these foods must be replenished to make them palatable; a brief soak in warm water is all it takes.

Legumes are the ultimate dried foods. Peas and beans can be used immediately, or stored for years. Their quality deteriorates with time, though, so store them in a cool, dry spot in an airtight container, and use the longest-stored legumes first.

Perhaps the most common dried food of all is pasta. We're so accustomed to the convenience, we don't even think of it as a preserved food. But it is — dried wheat paste (thus "pasta").

Frozen Foods

Freezing is the number one means of preserving foods if you happen to live at the North Pole. For the rest of us, it's an expensive convenience, a pleasure when it works, and a loss when it doesn't.

My husband remembers the shared freezer in the small town in Denmark where he grew up. It was a large unit at the grocer's, and you were given a ticket when you left your package there, like a deposit slip at the bank. The system was generally effective, but when the freezer was full, he remembers waiting a long time for a clerk to dig out his sausages.

A home freezer can enhance household economy if it is used wisely for all sorts of items such as sale and wholesale foods, garden produce, and breads, soups, and casseroles made ahead of time. My freezer is often packed with grain products such as bagels, whole wheat chapatis, and English muffins bought at the wholesaler; fruits such as papayas, bananas, and passion fruit from our trees; butter and an occasional piece of feta cheese bought in bulk; nuts and seeds that would turn rancid at room temperature; and purchased vegetables that freeze well, such as green peas, corn, and spinach.

The nutritional value of fresh produce is reduced somewhat by freezing, but not nearly as much as it is by canning. It's important to remember that you can only freeze and thaw fruits and vegetables *once* without doing them harm.

Canned Foods

Canned foods are easy to store and easy to use. It's a shame that food quality is compromised in the canning process, but it is. Anything canned has been cooked (and often overcooked). Vitamin and mineral contents are significantly reduced.

Still, some foods respond better than others to canning, and make life easy when you have them on hand. The cans I open usually contain whole peeled tomatoes or tomato paste, water chestnuts, bamboo shoots, and green chile peppers. Canned green chile salsa and enchilada sauce are also quite good.

Once opened, remove food from the can immediately; don't use the can to store leftover food (the metal may be reactive).

Bottled Foods

Glass jars hold the oil, vinegar, jam, tomato sauce, soy sauce, and sesame butter in my pantry. I like the clean feeling of glass, and being able to see the jar's contents. I like knowing that glass is stable and doesn't affect the contents of the jar. When complete glass recycling is established, I think we'll find it to be the most suitable material for circulating processed foods and beverages.

Two things to remember about bottled goods. First, anything bottled with liquid has been cooked, so a significant reduction in vitamins and minerals has occurred. Consider this when buying juice and baby food in particular. If you're buying these foods for nutritional content, remember that the food value has been reduced significantly by heat.

Second, most bottled products contain preservatives, particularly if they've been vacuum-packed. Look at the label on peanuts, hot peppers, and mayonnaise, for example. They read like alphabet soup. Many of these products wouldn't require preservatives if they had expiration dates on them, but most manufacturers are thus far not willing to put quality above their own convenience. As long as consumers are willing to buy chemical-laden products, companies will continue to produce them.

Vacuum-Packed Foods

In vacuum-packing, much of the oxygen in a jar, bag, or box is removed. Since it is the interaction of oxygen and food that spoils the product, reducing most of the oxygen slows deterioration. But complete removal of the oxygen is impossible, and for this reason, commercial products that are vacuum-packed either have expiration dates (as in the case of soymilk), or contain preservatives (as in the case of peanuts).

I like items with expiration dates. It gives me a sense of their lifespan, how fresh they are. I feel good about and prefer to support manufacturers who make freshness a priority.

Breaking Through

There's a strange phenomenon at play in kitchens across the country; I know because I discovered it in my own. It's really not a quirk of kitchens, it's a quirk of people.

Those of us who cook always love to try something new. It adds to the enjoyment of foodmaking, sparks our creativity, and keeps our tables interesting. At the same time, when looking through recipes and cookbooks, we tend to choose dishes that use the same, old, familiar ingredients. Where do we expect the newness to come from?

Speaking for myself, I notice that I regard unfamiliar ingredients with a mixture of excitement and aversion. (Psychologists call this an approach/avoidance response.) Here's an example. I'll read a recipe whose ingredients include "red curry paste." The dish sounds good, but I've never tried red curry paste, and I don't know where to get it. If I'm lucky enough to find it at the store, it might sit on my shelf for half a year before I decide to make the new dish. That's approach/avoidance.

I know many people who buy tofu once, then let it sit and rot in their refrigerator. "I didn't know what to do with it," they say later. (I did that myself.)

Yet one of the best things about cooking is the freedom we have to experiment. New dishes are made all the time. They are made by people who fire up their approach, and set their avoidance on the back burner. No one says mistakes won't be made, but who cares? By forging fearlessly ahead, we accelerate the learning process and realize gratifying results.

Where is this all leading? To ume plum vinegar and any other ingredients in this book you might not have tried yet. Follow the directions in the recipes and the arc of your learning curve will amaze you. I guarantee it.

Part Two:

Recipes for the Rest of Your Life

Soups

Soup is body, heart, and soul food. It's favored fare for toddlers, teenagers, truck drivers, opera singers, and my eighty-four-year-old uncle. Everyone responds to a good bowl of soup.

Each culture has its favorite, from Japanese miso to Portugese bean to Jewish chicken to Italian minestrone, to name a few. Why? Because the quickest route to quashing hunger is a hearty bowl of soup. Soup is also about as close to medicine as food gets. Who's to say what's medicine and what's food? Who's to say which needs healing most — body, heart, or soul?

From a chef's point of view, soup can be anything from a simple clear cupful to the heartiest potage, depending on its purpose. Whether it's intended to whet the appetite or satisfy it entirely, making soup is easy, and a great arena for creativity. When I first discovered red lentils, I realized just how easy it can be. The bright, fragile beans cook in 20 minutes, and make a moderately thick base for soups as varied as your own imagination. My favorite, Golden Soup, pairs red lentils with carrots, zucchini, parsley, and potatoes in a hearty broth.

In addition to their gastronomic and rejuvenating properties, soups provide the creative cook with a spot to put a little extra protein or fiber or leftover bits and pieces from previous meals. The last corner of hard cheese or previously steamed beans or an uneaten baked potato are all candidates for the soup pot. Not-so-fresh but still edible carrots, onions, cabbages, and cauliflowers gravitate in the same direction. This is the practical, whimsical, and traditional way good soup has always been made.

A NOTE ON STOCKS

I've always used vegetable bouillon cubes and the Swiss brand Hugli is my favorite. Many a time I've decided to make my own stock, and many a bag of vegetable scraps and peelings has accumulated for that purpose in my refrigerator. But truth be told, I've never — not once — gone through with it. Instead, I'll open a package of Hugli cubes, enjoying the tiny box and its well-wrapped contents, and every time I've been perfectly satisfied with the results. Chalk it up to laziness . . . or lack of inspiration with onionskins.

Homestyle Mushroom Soup

My husband calls this "good, down-home soup." I call it "clean." What we mean is that this is not a sophisticated recipe. It's everyday fare made with ordinary ingredients. Potatoes and onions form a hearty base for the large slices of mushrooms, which are the focal point of the soup. The potatoes break down; the mushrooms stand out. It's as simple as that.

I large onion, diced

3½ cups peeled, diced russet potato (about 3 large)

3¼ cups water

I vegetable bouillon cube

½ pound sliced mushrooms

I tablespoon olive oil

1½ tablespoons soy sauce

1½ tablespoons garbanzo flour (or whole wheat flour)

2 to 2½ teaspoons seasoned salt

2 tablespoons minced parsley

Put the onions and potatoes in a soup pot with the water and bouillon cube. Bring to a boil, covered, then reduce heat to a simmer and continue to cook, covered, until the potatoes are done.

Wash and slice the mushrooms, and sauté them separately in the olive oil. Stir frequently, since you're not using much oil. When the mushrooms begin to release their liquid, add the soy sauce. Push the mushrooms to the sides of the pan, and whisk the flour into the liquid in the middle. Whisk it well, adding liquid by the quarter-cup from the soup pot as it becomes necessary. Cook this, stirring in the mushrooms from the sides of the pan, for about 3 minutes, then turn off the heat.

When the potatoes are tender, mash them with a potato masher. Add the mushroom mixture. Add the seasoned salt to taste. Heat through. Garnish with parsley just before serving.

Yield: 4 to 6 servings

Curried Carrot Soup

This soup surprises people who think they don't like cooked carrots. The carrots form the base of a bright-orange, chunky, mildly spicy, nut-topped potage that hits the spot. A bit of couscous added at the end thickens the broth. When I serve Carrot Soup on a menu that includes another dish containing chopped nuts, I omit the soup's almond garnish and use parsley instead.

½ cup almonds

2 tablespoons butter, or olive oil

2¼ pounds carrots, coarsely
    chopped (about 6 very large)

3 stalks celery, chopped

1 large onion, chopped

1 tablespoon (optional) very finely
    grated fresh ginger

¾ teaspoon quality curry powder

A pinch each of nutmeg and
    cayenne pepper

6 cups vegetable bouillon

¼ cup couscous, uncooked

Salt and freshly ground black
    pepper to taste

¼ cup minced parsley

Bake the almonds in an unpreheated toaster oven for about 12 minutes at 350 degrees. Once they've cooled, chop coarsely.

Melt the butter or olive oil in a soup pot and sauté the carrots, celery, and onions until the onion is soft. Then add ginger (if used), curry, nutmeg, cayenne, and bouillon. Simmer until the carrots are tender.

Carefully blenderize about half the soup, filling the blender no more than half full, and starting on a low speed with the lid on loosely. Return blended soup to the pot. Add the couscous. Heat for 10 minutes, then season with pepper and salt to taste. Just before serving, add the parsley.

Serve each bowl garnished liberally with the chopped almonds.

Yield: 6 to 8 servings

Emerald Soup

For ease of preparation and elegant appearance, this is dream soup incarnate. It's light, flavorful, and sets the stage for a real culinary event. Garnished with a nasturtium, this soup is a preview of Spring itself. (Can it be true, then, that it's based on frozen peas?)

1 medium onion, finely chopped

2 tablespoons butter

1½ tablespoons whole wheat pastry flour

2 pinches white pepper

3¾ cups hot vegetable bouillon

½ teaspoon honey

4⅔ cups frozen green peas (about 2½ 10-ounce packages)

Salt and pepper to taste (if desired; I don't add any)

One nasturtium per bowl for garnish (or a dollop of sour cream per serving for garnish)

Sauté the onion in butter over medium-low heat until it is transparent, then add the flour and mix it in with the flat edge of a spatula or wooden spoon. Stir constantly for 3 minutes to cook the flour. Lumps are okay.

Add the pepper, the hot bouillon, and the honey; simmer 5 minutes, covered. Add 4 cups of the peas and remove the soup from the heat (reserve the remaining peas; they go in whole later).

Purée the soup in the blender, then strain it. (Don't omit the straining; the texture it yields is one of this soup's best qualities.)

Return the strained soup to the pot and heat it through, but don't overcook it. Overcooked, the soup loses its beautiful emerald color and turns a drab olive green. Try to have people at the table the moment the soup is hot. If they're not, remove the soup from the heat and leave it uncovered until serving time; it's better slightly cooled than overcooked. Put about 2 tablespoons whole peas in each serving bowl and ladle the soup atop them. Garnish and serve immediately.

Yield: 4 servings

I love this house. We built it
in four distinct parts, each as we
could afford. Every room has its
own personality. I don't think the
kitchen is in the middle of the
house by accident – it's the hub.
Days can go by before I step into
the "living room;" but that's never
the case with the kitchen. I guess
it's a "living kitchen." And I'm
not the only one living there.

Golden Soup

If I had to choose a favorite soup this would be it, for the ease, the taste, and the way it looks. All this, with little or no added fat.

6 cups water

2 vegetable bouillon cubes

I cup red lentils (they're called "red" even though they're orange)

I½ cups diced onion

2 cloves pressed garlic

½ teaspoon turmeric

I bay leaf

I cup diced celery

I½ cups diced carrot

I cup diced potato

I½ cups diced zucchini

¼ to ½ cup minced parsley

¼ to ½ cup nutritional yeast (optional but recommended)

I tablespoon extra-virgin olive oil (optional)

Seasoned salt and pepper to taste

Bring the water to a boil in a large soup pot and add the bouillon cubes.

Wash the lentils thoroughly in several changes of water until they stop foaming, then drain and add to the pot. Also add the onion, garlic, turmeric, and bay leaf. Simmer 25 minutes.

Add the celery, carrot, and potato; simmer 10 minutes more, then add the zucchini and simmer another 10 minutes.

Add the parsley and whisk in the nutritional yeast and olive oil, if desired. Add seasoned salt and pepper; serve immediately.

Yield: 6 servings

Fiesta Pumpkin Soup

You can make this colorful soup with pumpkin, butternut, or banana squash —
they're all good. And plan to make leftovers; it's even better the second day (especially
with cornbread or quesadillas and green salad for lunch).

3 to 3½ cups water*

**1 small jalapeño pepper, chopped
(optional)**

½ cup chopped onion

**1½ pounds pumpkin squash (about
3½ cups, seeded, peeled,
and chopped)**

2 cloves pressed garlic

½ cup chopped green pepper

¾ cup chopped zucchini

**1½ tablespoons riso (rice-shaped
pasta), uncooked**

**⅓ cup chopped parsley (Italian
parsley preferred)**

1½ teaspoons seasoned salt

¼ teaspoon thyme

1 tablespoon soy sauce

1½ teaspoons extra-virgin olive oil

1 teaspoon ground cumin seed

**½ cup corn, cut from cob or frozen
and thawed**

½ to ¾ teaspoons salt to taste

¼ cup chopped red bell pepper

**½ cup cooked kidney beans
(canned or leftover beans
are fine)**

Put the water, jalapeño pepper, onion, pumpkin, and
garlic in a large soup pot and bring to a boil. (*The
amount of water you use will determine the heartiness
of the soup. If you want it thick, creamy, and stewlike,
use less; for a lighter soup, use more.)

Reduce heat and simmer 30 minutes until pumpkin
is tender. Mash coarsely.

Add the green pepper, zucchini, and riso. Cook 15
minutes, then add remaining ingredients. Heat
through and taste. Add salt and pepper if desired.

Yield: 4 to 6 servings

Thai Vegetable Soup

Fresh with vegetables and rich with coconut milk, this soup provides a light and unusual first course before an Asian or Indonesian meal. Make it as mild or as spicy as you like with cayenne pepper.

1 tablespoon mild oil,
    such as canola

8 to 12 cloves pressed garlic

1½ cups chopped onion

1 teaspoon finely grated organic
    lemon zest (yellow part only)

4 cups water

2 vegetable bouillon cubes

1 cup carrot, cut in a fine,
    1-inch-long julienne

1½ cups green beans, cut in
    1-inch-long slivers

1 cup previously cooked potato
    cubes (leftover, baked, diced,
    or steamed)

1 cup chopped Chinese cabbage
    (or green cabbage)

1 cup coconut milk

Cayenne pepper to taste

¼ cup chopped Chinese parsley
    (or 1 minced green onion)
    for garnish

1 lemon or lime

Heat the oil in a soup pot and sauté the garlic and chopped onion. When the onion becomes transparent, add the lemon zest and sauté briefly until fragrant. Add the water and the bouillon cubes; bring to a boil, then reduce heat to a simmer and add the carrot, green beans, potato, and cabbage. Simmer uncovered until the vegetables are tender (about 10 minutes), then add the coconut milk. Keep a sharp eye on the pot. If the soup comes to a boil, the coconut milk may curdle, so just heat it through. Add cayenne to taste, garnish with the Chinese parsley or green onion, and serve immediately while the beans are still bright green. Offer lemon or lime wedges at the table.

Yield: 4 to 6 servings

Lima Bean Chowder

Lima beans and potatoes, blended to a smooth consistency, make a creamy yet dairy-free base for this soup. The lima flavor is subtle but the creaminess is not. Once the base is made add your choice of seasonal vegetables. We like fresh corn, cut from the cob, red peppers, and spinach. But for a good basic soup, even carrots, cabbage, and frozen green peas would do the job. (If you do choose these vegetables, dice the carrots and cabbage finely so they are tender at the same time as the peas.)

**2 cups dried lima beans,
    soaked overnight**

7 cups water

**2 medium potatoes, peeled
    and diced**

2 bay leaves

3 cloves pressed garlic

2 tablespoons extra-virgin olive oil

I large onion or leek, chopped

3 tablespoons soy sauce

I½ tablespoons white wine vinegar

2 teaspoons salt

2 cups corn, cut from the cob

I diced sweet red pepper

I cup finely chopped spinach

Drain the soaked lima beans, rinse them thoroughly, and place in a soup pot with the water, the potatoes, the bay leaves, and the garlic. Bring the water to a boil, skim off the foam, reduce the heat to a simmer, and cook, covered, I½ hours.

Heat the olive oil in a skillet and sauté the onion or leek until it's well done; reserve.

When the lima beans and potatoes are done, blenderize the soup until absolutely smooth and return it to the soup pot. Add soy sauce, vinegar, salt, and the sautéed onions or leeks. Also add the corn, red pepper, and spinach or other vegetables of choice. Heat through until the spinach is wilted and everything is hot.

Yield: 6 servings

Three-Bean Soup

I make Three-Bean Soup when I have other kitchen projects going — if I'm baking bread, for example, and am in the kitchen anyway. The soup is a simple long-simmering pot of barley, beans, and assorted vegetables. It doesn't take much attention, but it likes you to be there to add a few ingredients every half hour or so. This is satisfying rainy-day fare.

6 cups water
⅓ cup barley
⅓ cup kidney beans, unsoaked and uncooked
1½ cups chopped onion
6 cloves chopped or pressed garlic
⅓ cup brown lentils
⅓ cup black-eyed peas, uncooked
1 cup finely chopped small, waxy potatoes
1 cup chopped carrot
2 cups water
2 to 2½ teaspoons salt (or enough to taste)
2 tablespoons soy sauce
2 tablespoons red wine vinegar
2 tablespoons extra-virgin olive oil
1 cup chopped peppers (a combination of red and green is nice)
½ teaspoon marjoram leaves
½ teaspoon basil leaves
¼ teaspoon allspice
¼ teaspoon black pepper
1 cup finely chopped parsley

Put the water, barley, kidney beans, onion, and 2 cloves chopped garlic in a large pot; bring to a boil, then reduce the heat to a simmer, cover the pot, and set the timer for 30 minutes.

Add the lentils, black-eyed peas, and 2 more cloves chopped garlic. Set the time for 30 minutes again.

When the timer rings, add the potato, carrot, additional water, and the remaining garlic. Set the timer one last time, for 30 minutes.

Add the remaining ingredients, reserving ¼ cup parsley for a last-minute garnish. Cook until the peppers are tender, 5 to 10 minutes. The soup can be served immediately or aged for a couple of hours. (It tastes best after it has aged.) Garnish with remaining parsley just before serving.

Yield: 8 servings

Miso Soup Plus

This is not a recipe for traditional miso soup, but it is a light, colorful, and satisfying potage based on a unique Japanese food. This dish is not a hearty meal-in-a-bowl like Lentil Soup; it is a delicate announcement of goodness, and of more to come.

½ cup water

2 tablespoons hijiki

5 cups water

2 vegetable bouillon cubes

3 tablespoons small pasta shapes such as wheels or shells, or ½ cup finely cubed firm, silken tofu

Half of a small cauliflower (chop to make 1½ cups cauli-florets)

2 tablespoons barley miso or brown rice miso

1 medium carrot, cut in a fine julienne

1 large leaf of chard, or 4 spinach leaves, cut in slivers

3 green onions, chopped finely

Boil the water and pour over the hijiki in a small bowl.

Bring the 5 cups water to boil in a small soup pot, add the bouillon cubes, and decide whether you will be using pasta or tofu in the soup. If pasta, add to the water when it boils.

Add the cauliflower to the soup. Lift the hijiki from its soaking water and put it in the soup too, discarding the soaking water. When the soup boils, reduce heat to a simmer. Put the miso in a small bowl and add ¼ cup of the boiling bouillon to it. Mix to make a smooth paste, and add it to the soup pot. (It is important not to boil the soup after the miso is added. Miso contains valuable enzymes that are destroyed by boiling.) By this time, the pasta should be done. Add the carrots, the chard (or spinich) and the tofu, if you're using it. When the tofu is heated through, add the green onions. Serve the soup immediately, while the vegetables are still firm.

Yield: 5 first-course servings

Salads

At my house, salads are a staple; we savor them almost nightly, and rarely tire of even the simplest lettuce and tomato combination if the vegetables are garden-fresh. Because leafy salads are simple to make and don't require much in the way of recipes, this chapter focuses more on specialty salads that include rice, pasta, and beans as well as raw and cooked vegetables. But first, a few words about the essential green salad.

Salad ingredients require special treatment from the seed to the salad bowl. Once harvested, freshness is all. Pay attention to what's in season and don't settle for last year's apples or potatoes if you have other options. Also, unless the idea of eating pesticide residue appeals to you, request organically grown produce. The more it's requested, the more will be grown.

It's wonderful to eat fresh, raw greens. I think the reappearance of long-forgotten greens like arugula (or rocket) and chicory is timely, not trendy. It's a pleasure to have bitter greens other than parsley to select. Here on Maui, mixed baby greens ready for the table are sold by the pound. It's a simple (although expensive) pleasure to taste smooth butter lettuce, sweet purple basil, and ruffly kale leaves side by side.

At our table, the salad dressing is more variable than the salad ingredients. With frequent changes of dressing, we're quite content to eat the same assortment of vegetables, generally a combination of lettuce, arugula, carrots, sprouts, and whatever else the garden may offer, night after night. To our taste, freshness counts more than variety.

House Salad

I never measure anything when I make our nightly salad. I just wash, chop, and grate vegetables until the salad is finished. I did measure (for once), so it could be printed here. Its striking green, black, orange, and crimson color scheme, and the contrasting textures of hijiki, avocado, and crunchy beet are particularly appealing. Since salads that contain avocado do not store well, serve the avocado on the side if you think you'll have leftovers.

10 cups loosely packed salad greens

2 cups alfalfa sprouts

⅔ cup carrot, scrubbed and sliced thinly on the diagonal

⅔ cup peeled, finely grated raw beet

⅓ cup hijiki soaked in 3 cups hot water for 30 minutes, drained, and tossed with 1 tablespoon soy sauce

1 cup avocado, sliced or diced

3 tablespoon toasted sunflower seeds (optional)

When all the vegetables are prepared, they can either be tossed together or arranged attractively to show off the vibrant colors. I usually toss the greens, sprouts, and half the avocado, then arrange the beet, carrots, hijiki, and the remaining avocado and sunflower seeds atop. Chunks of previously baked potato are good to add, as are all chilled, steamed vegetables.

There's not a dressing in this book that wouldn't make a feast of this salad.

Yield: 6 to 8 servings

French Salad

The French "everyday" salad is simple to prepare and a real treat to eat. The dressing is made in the bottom of the salad bowl; crisp, green lettuce leaves and tomato chunks are tossed atop, and the whole thing is mixed and served immediately. It's a masterpiece of freshness.

¼ cup extra-virgin olive oil

1 teaspoon Dijon mustard

1 tablespoon white wine (or champagne) vinegar

⅓ teaspoon salt (or to taste)

8 cups fresh lettuce leaves, preferably from the heart of the lettuce

2 small, ripe tomatoes

Black pepper to grind at the table

Whisk together the oil, mustard, vinegar, and salt in the bottom of the (preferably wooden) salad bowl.

Be sure the lettuce is clean and dry. If the leaves are small, serve them whole; otherwise tear them gently. Wash, dry, and cut the tomatoes in thick wedges, then in half.

Toss the salad with the dressing and serve at once. Pass the black pepper grinder.

Yield: 4 servings

Cauliflower Salad Supreme

As far as I'm concerned, this salad is the best thing that ever happened to cauliflower. To begin, the vegetable is cut in thick slices and steamed. Once cool, it's topped with a lively mixture of finely chopped Kalamata olives, tomatoes, and capers, all bathed in olive oil and balsamic vinegar. The dressing permeates the cauliflower and flows through to the bed of lettuce underneath. Make this for those you love.

I large cauliflower (2½ to 3 pounds)
4 tablespoons capers, drained
½ cup pitted and chopped Kalamata olives
I½ cups finely chopped tomato
½ cup extra-virgin olive oil
2 tablespoons balsamic vinegar
½ teaspoon salt
I large head lettuce
⅓ of a long cucumber (Japanese or English)

Trim the leaves from the cauliflower, but do not cut out the core, (it holds the slices together). Cut the cauliflower into 8 equal slices (about ¾-inch thick apiece), taking care to keep them intact. Lay the slices in a steamer and steam until tender, about 20 minutes. Remove the steamer from the pot to cool the cauliflower.

Combine the capers, olives, tomato, oil, vinegar, and salt in a small bowl; reserve.

Wash and dry the lettuce; tear it into bite-sized pieces and place on 4 salad plates. Slice the cucumber thinly — you'll need about 20 slices.

When the cauliflower has cooled, arrange the slices atop the lettuce attractively, 2 slices to a plate. Tuck the cucumber slices around the cauliflower. Spoon the tomato mixture over the cauliflower, using all of the dressing. Serve at room temperature.

Yield: 4 servings

Chinese Cabbage Salad

I found the inspiration for this recipe in a magazine years ago, and adapted it for a seminar I was catering. It was so popular, it turned into a regular on my menu. Combining ramen noodles with Chinese cabbage works beautifully, and basing the salad's dressing on the ramen seasoning packet was brilliant. I offer here my rendition, with compliments to the recipe's unknown originator.

1 package ramen soup mix
5 cups shredded Chinese cabbage
4 green onions, finely chopped
2 tablespoons toasted sesame seeds
3 tablespoons rice vinegar
1 tablespoon honey
1½ tablespoons mild oil, such as canola
1½ teaspoons toasted sesame oil*
½ teaspoon white pepper
¼ teaspoon salt
½ cup toasted, slivered almonds, or toasted cashew nuts

> ***Toasted sesame oil, also known as aromatic, or dark sesame oil, has a unique, pervasive flavor and fragrance. It is a common ingredient in Asian cookery, and may be purchased at an Asian or natural foods store.**

Remove ramen noodles from the package and break them apart with your hands. Put them in a bowl and pour boiling water over them until they soften, about 5 minutes. Drain and rinse with cold water until they are cool; store the noodles in cold water while you chop the vegetables.

Toast the sesame seeds and nuts about 10 minutes, or until fragrant, at 300 degrees in the toaster oven (keep them separated).

Shred the cabbage finely and place it, the chopped green onions, and the toasted sesame seeds in a salad bowl. Drain the noodles thoroughly, shaking excess water from the strainer vigorously, and add the noodles to the salad.

To make the dressing, open the seasoning packet which comes with the ramen and place contents in a small mixing bowl. Add the vinegar, honey, oils, pepper, and salt. Whisk thoroughly and pour dressing over the salad. Toss thoroughly, and garnish the salad with toasted nuts.

Yield: 4 to 6 servings

Chinese Cashew Salad

I often want a green salad on the menu even if I'm serving Asian food, and this dish, which is modeled after Chinese Chicken Salad, grew out of that desire.

You have choices here, first with dressings. If you like sweet and sour, try the Plum Sauce Dressing. Otherwise, go with the Light. You may also choose to include or omit the Chinese Tofu Chunks. Plum sauce and powdered Thai ginger are available in Asian markets.

For the Salad:

5 cups shredded romaine lettuce

**2 cups coarsely chopped
    bean sprouts**

⅔ cup celery, sliced on the diagonal

½ can sliced water chestnuts

**1 green onion, thinly sliced
    on the diagonal**

⅓ cup toasted cashews

Chinese Tofu Chunks (optional)

For the Plum Sauce Dressing:

2 tablespoons plum sauce

2 tablespoons lemon juice

1 tablespoon toasted sesame oil

For the Light Dressing:

2 tablespoons rice vinegar

**2 tablespoons mild oil, such as
    canola**

2 teaspoons toasted sesame oil

2 teaspoons soy sauce

2 teaspoons honey

**½ teaspoon finely grated fresh
    ginger (or ¼ teaspoon
    dried ginger)**

Pinch of salt, pinch of white pepper

Combine salad ingredients in a mixing bowl, reserving a few cashews for garnish. Whisk dressing ingredients together separately. Immediately before serving, toss the dressing with the salad, and garnish with the reserved cashews.

Yield: 4 servings

For the Chinese Tofu Chunks:

½ pound firm tofu

2 tablespoons soy sauce

1½ teaspoons toasted sesame oil

1½ teaspoons finely grated, fresh ginger

⅛ teaspoon powdered Thai ginger (optional)

Drain the tofu in a strainer for at least 5 minutes, then dry it thoroughly with a clean towel. Slice it thinly (about ½-inch thick), then cut it into 1-inch squares. Cut the squares in half on the diagonal, to make small triangles.

Combine soy sauce, sesame oil, and ginger(s) in a small baking dish, add the tofu triangles, and toss. Bake until all the liquid evaporates, and the tofu has a golden crust. (A toaster oven is perfect for this small amount.) In my oven, the process takes 30 minutes at 350 degrees, and an additional 25 minutes at 375 degrees. Turn the tofu after about 40 minutes of baking. Cool thoroughly before tossing into the salad.

Kalamata Coleslaw

As much as I used to love mayonnaise-drenched coleslaw, I find I prefer the lighter, vinaigrette-dressed versions such as this, which is flavored with olives, parsley, and sweet red peppers. The secret of good coleslaw is thinly cut cabbage. Chewy vegetable that it is, cabbage requires a fine cut to make a delicate salad.

1 pound green cabbage (about 6 cups shredded)

2 green onions

½ cup pitted and chopped Kalamata olives

⅓ cup minced Italian parsley

2 tablespoons extra-virgin olive oil

2 large cloves garlic, minced or pressed

1 large sweet red pepper, cut in fine, inch-long slivers

1 tablespoon soymilk or milk

1 tablespoon red wine vinegar

¼ teaspoon Dijon mustard

½ teaspoon dried basil leaves

½ teaspoon salt (or to taste)

Shred the cabbage very finely with a knife (not in a food processor) and put it in a large bowl. Trim the green onions and slice them lengthwise, then chop them and add them to the bowl. Add the olives and parsley.

Heat 1 tablespoon of the oil in a large skillet. When it's hot, add the garlic and the red pepper. Sauté over high heat for about 30 seconds, then add to the salad. Use a rubber scraper to get all the oil from the pan.

In a separate bowl, whisk together the remaining tablespoon of olive oil, the soymilk, vinegar, mustard, basil, and salt. Toss this dressing with the salad. Serve at room temperature.

Yield: 4 to 6 servings

Cold Soba Salad
with Celery, Shiitake, and Sesame

Cold noodle salads are a favorite in Hawaii because they are refreshing and easy to make. Soba (buckwheat) noodles hold their shape in a salad particularly well. This dish is decidedly Oriental in flavor and appearance and makes a choice addition to an Asian buffet. It's also good on its own as a cool, satisfying lunch.

½ **pound soba noodles**
I cup vegetable bouillon
4 large shiitake mushrooms (dried)
2 tablespoons sesame seeds
I½ tablespoons soy sauce
2 tablespoons rice vinegar
I tablespoon toasted sesame oil
I tablespoon mild oil, such as canola
½ **teaspoon Tabasco sauce**
½ **teaspoon honey**
I½ teaspoons finely grated ginger root
3 large cloves pressed garlic
I½ teaspoons sherry
I teaspoon salt
½ **cup chopped Chinese parsley**
½ **cup celery, cut in fine julienne**

Bring a large pot of unsalted water to boil and add the noodles. Separately, heat the vegetable bouillon. Divide the hot bouillon in half. Put ½ cup in a large mixing bowl, where the dressing will be made, and in the remaining ½ cup place the dried mushrooms, stem side up. Toast the sesame seeds for 10 minutes at 300 degrees in a toaster oven (no preheating necessary).

Add the soy sauce, vinegar, oils, Tabasco, honey, ginger, garlic, sherry, and salt to the bouillon. Whisk thoroughly.

When the noodles are done, rinse with cold water until cool, then drain well, shaking all the water out. Add the cold noodles to the dressing; also add the Chinese parsley, celery, and half of the sesame seeds.

Remove the dried mushrooms from their soaking liquid, squeeze them gently to remove excess liquid, and cut them in l-inch slivers. Add them to the salad and toss thoroughly. Garnish with the remaining sesame seeds and serve.

Yield: 3 to 4 servings for lunch or 6 servings for a buffet

Oriental Noodle Salad

For its lightness, simplicity, and near-addictive good taste, I make this recipe often. It's excellent fresh and very good the next day too, which makes it a natural for parties and picnics.

½ **pound thin Chinese egg noodles* or soba (buckwheat) noodles, cooked until tender (not a moment longer)**

2 **cloves pressed garlic**

¼ **cup soy sauce**

1½ **tablespoons toasted sesame oil**

1½ **tablespoons mild oil, such as canola**

½ **teaspoon Tabasco sauce (or more to taste)**

2 **tablespoons red wine vinegar**

1½ **cups finely diced broccoli florets, blanched**

3 **tablespoons minced green onions**

¾ **to 1 cup finely diced sweet red pepper**

1 **cup coarsely chopped bean sprouts**

Put 3 quarts of water on to boil.

In a wide, shallow bowl, combine the garlic, soy sauce, sesame oil, mild oil, Tabasco, and vinegar.

Dice the broccoli florets while the water comes to a boil; then prepare the other vegetables. When the water boils, add the noodles. Chinese egg noodles cook quickly — in about 2 minutes; buckwheat noodles take longer, 8 to 10 minutes. Just before the noodles are done, toss in the broccoli for 30 to 60 seconds.

Drain the noodle/broccoli mixture and rinse in several changes of cold water until they are cool. Drain in a colander, shaking vigorously to get all the water out, then add the noodles and broccoli to the dressing. Toss with clean fingers.

Toss in the green onions, the red pepper, and the bean sprouts.

Yield: 4 servings

. . . .
*The Chinese egg noodles I've found are called "pancit canton." They are made in the Phillipines and unfortunately contain yellow dye which I don't like, but the noodles have a great taste.
. . . .

Mexican Rice Salad

I've been making marinated rice salads for years — they're perfect with Mexican food — but only recently have I included black beans. Here, the beans are marinated first, making them flavorful and attractive; then they're tossed with the cooled rice and brightly colored vegetables. The result is a particularly delectable salad which also provides complete protein. Leftover rice finds a satisfying second home here. You may also substitute a cup of fresh corn, cut off the cob, for the black beans. This makes a lighter salad, and one that can be served with a Mexican meal that already contains beans.

¾ cup black (turtle) beans, uncooked

⅓ cup extra-virgin olive oil

⅓ cup white wine vinegar

1½ teaspoons salt

4 cups cooked brown rice

1 large tomato, diced (and drained, if it's watery)

1 finely chopped green pepper

½ cup chopped Chinese parsley or one minced green onion, if preferred

1 medium lime for garnish (optional)

Soak the beans in 4 cups water for 8 hours or overnight, then drain; cook, covered, 1½ to 2 hours in fresh, unsalted water. Be sure to cook them at a simmer, so they don't break apart. Taste for doneness after 1½ hours; actual cooking time will depend upon the age of the beans.

Drain the cooked beans thoroughly and combine with the oil, vinegar, and salt. Let them marinate for at least 30 minutes. Chop the tomato, green pepper, and Chinese parsley (or onion).

Toss cooled rice and chopped vegetables with the marinated beans. Garnish with wedges of lime if desired.

Yield: 6 servings

Curried Rice Salad

Light, festive, and fruity, this salad is beautiful on a buffet table, especially if you have a dozen or so small, edible flowers like impatiens or begonias to garnish the platter. Cool rice, sliced bananas, currants, and shredded coconut are mixed and mounded on a bed of lettuce, doused with a silky golden sauce, and topped with toasted cashew nuts. The result is a remarkably low-fat yet rich-tasting dish. Try it with Indian food.

For the Rice:

3 cups cooked brown rice, cooled
4 small bananas, sliced
½ cup dried currants
⅓ cup dried, unsweetened coconut
8 to 10 fresh, green lettuce leaves

For the Dressing:

⅔ cup plain yogurt (non-fat is fine)
1½ teaspoons quality curry powder
1 tablespoon honey
Pinch of ginger
¼ teaspoon salt

For the Top:

½ cup raw cashew nuts
A dozen small edible flowers, or
    sprigs of fresh mint (optional)

Roast the cashews in the toaster oven for about 10 minutes at 300 degrees until lightly golden.

Line a serving platter with the lettuce leaves. Combine rice, bananas, currants, and coconut. Toss gently, then mound atop the lettuce in a dome or oval shape, smoothing the surface with a rubber spatula or your hands.

Combine dressing ingredients and mix until smooth. Pour over rice attractively and garnish with the nuts and flowers or mint, if desired.

Yield: 4 servings

Hawaii is known for many
things, among them the lucky
little lizards known as geckos.
They flourish in our kitchen,
and congregate on the spice
shelves. I've found their eggs in
the utensil crock. Geckos are
not shy; they talk, eat, even
fight in public. They rarely
walk on the floor. (Who
would, when you can walk on
walls, windows, and ceilings?)

Walnut Beet Salad

This very simple salad — three ingredients plus a dressing — is more than the sum of its parts. When tender crimson beets meet the crunch of shredded romaine and richly toasted walnuts, something new happens, and it's something worth tasting.

2 medium-large beets
1 large head romaine
1 cup walnuts
½ cup plus 1 tablespoon Honey-Mustard Vinaigrette (page 52)
2 tablespoons raspberry vinegar (or balsamic vinegar)

Cut the beets in half and steam them until tender, about 40 minutes. Cool them in a bowl of water, slip off the skins and dice them (you should have about 2½ cups).

Toast the walnuts until fragrant and crunchy, 10 to 12 minutes in a 300-degree toaster oven that hasn't been preheated. Chop the toasted walnuts coarsely.

Wash, dry, and cut the romaine at half-inch intervals across the width of the leaves, then twice lengthwise, making coarse, bite-sized shreds (you should have about 10 cups).

Combine the Honey-Mustard Vinaigrette with vinegar in a large bowl, and just before serving, add dressing to the beets, romaine, and about ¾ cup of the walnuts. Toss thoroughly, and place in serving bowl. Garnish with remaining walnuts and serve.

Yield: 6 to 8 servings

Caponata Pasta Salad

This salad is particularly suitable for a buffet table or a first course. It's also an ideal side dish.

1 large round eggplant

7 tablespoons extra-virgin olive oil

12 ounces penne (thin pasta tubes, cut diagonally on the ends)

3 small zucchini (each 5 to 6 inches long, 1-inch diameter)

1 red pepper

1 green pepper

1 clove pressed garlic

½ teaspoon salt

⅔ cup finely chopped fresh basil leaves

2 to 3 tablespoons capers, with a bit of their juice

2 tablespoons red wine vinegar

2 teaspoons balsamic vinegar

¾ teaspoon salt (or to taste)

¼ teaspoon pepper

½ cup freshly grated Parmesan cheese (optional)

Slice the eggplant into ¾-inch slabs, brush with 1 tablespoon of the oil, and bake 30 minutes or until fork-tender, at 350 degrees.

Cook the pasta until done in 5 quarts boiling water with ¾ tablespoon salt. Cut the zucchini into ¼-inch rounds (you should have 2 cups) and dice the peppers. Heat 3 tablespoons of the oil until very hot in a large, heavy skillet, and stir-fry the peppers and zucchini for 3 minutes over high heat; add the garlic. Stir-fry 1 to 2 minutes more, then put the vegetables and all pan juices in a large mixing bowl. Sprinkle with ½ teaspoon salt.

Add the chopped basil and the capers. When the eggplant is tender, chop it; add it and the well-drained pasta, to the bowl.

Pour the remaining oil, the vinegars, the Parmesan if desired, and the remaining salt and pepper over the pasta. Toss well and season to taste. The dish is ready to serve warm, as it is, or at room temperature.

Yield: 6 servings

Mexi-Maui Salad

I *like to serve this unusual salad in large, shallow, individual bowls lined first with crisp green lettuce, then a scoop of steaming brown rice. With the salad on top, it makes a festive presentation.*

2 cups cooked kidney beans,
    drained
½ cup salsa
2 tablespoons minced red or
    sweet onion
1 clove pressed garlic
2 tablespoons chopped Chinese
    parsley (optional)
¼ cup extra-virgin olive oil
¼ cup red wine vinegar
½ teaspoon salt
¼ teaspoon cumin powder
¼ teaspoon paprika
¼ teaspoon dried oregano leaves
2 cups cubed avocado

Combine the beans, salsa, onion, garlic, parsley (if using), oil, vinegar, salt, and spices. Allow to marinate for 30 minutes, then gently toss in the avocado. Serve immediately at room temperature.

Yield: 4 servings

Black-Eyed Pea Salad

I think black-eyed peas are the tastiest of all beans, with a moist, creamy texture second to none. They also cook relatively quickly, even without presoaking. This salad is good over rice, in a burrito (drain off the dressing first), or best of all, as part of a Southern banquet with juicy baked yams, cornbread, breaded tofu cutlets, and a tossed green salad. At such a feast, blackberry pie makes the perfect dessert.

1½ cups dried black-eyed peas
¼ cup white wine vinegar
⅓ cup extra-virgin olive oil
½ cup minced Italian parsley
½ cup minced red onion (optional)
1 teaspoon salt
¼ teaspoon black pepper
1 tablespoon mild oil, such as canola
1 sweet red bell pepper, minced
2 cloves pressed garlic

Bring the peas to a boil in plenty of fresh, unsalted water, then reduce the heat to a simmer. If the heat is too high, the beans will fall apart. Cook until tender, about 50 minutes.

Drain the beans and mix them with the vinegar, olive oil, parsley, onion, salt, and pepper.

In a large, heavy skillet, heat the oil until very hot. Add the pepper and garlic and cook them quickly, stirring constantly, for 30 seconds. Use a rubber spatula to add the vegetables and oil to the beans. Toss gently and serve at room temperature.

Yield: 4 to 6 servings

Thai Salad

Sweet, salty, tart, pungent, crisp, crunchy, soft — this salad covers a lot of territory. If you like variety and strong tastes, you'll find them gathered here in one light, appealing dish.

For an authentic and outrageous Asian meal, serve Thai Salad on a menu with Spicy Fried Rice, Curried Tofu with Green Beans and Basil, and Oriental Noodle Salad. Fresh mangos (or citrus sorbet) are perfect for dessert.

⅓ cup unsulphured dried apricots*

I head romaine lettuce, washed and dried

I cup seeded, sliced cucumber (peeled if desired)

I cup halved tomato wedges

2 cups bean sprouts, coarsely chopped

¾ cup Chinese parsley, chopped

½ cup roasted peanuts (salted or not), coarsely chopped

I recipe Peanut Dressing, below

Dice the dried apricots and pour boiling water over them just to cover. Let them stand until soft but not mushy, about 15 minutes; drain. (Drink the soaking liquid — it's delicious.)

Make the Peanut Dressing. Chop the lettuce; you should have about 8 cups. Just before serving, combine the lettuce, vegetables, apricots, dressing, and half the peanuts. Place in a salad bowl that is just the right size (the salad should reach the top of the bowl). Sprinkle peanuts over the top and serve immediately. Note that the salad becomes soggy if it sits for long.

Yield: 4 to 6 servings

For the Peanut Dressing:

4 tablespoons peanut butter

4 tablespoons mild oil, such as canola

2 tablespoons plus 2 teaspoons soy sauce

2 tablespoons honey

I tablespoon plus I teaspoon white wine vinegar

I teaspoon toasted sesame oil

Salt and cayenne pepper to taste

Blenderize or whisk together the peanut butter and oil. When thoroughly blended, whisk in the remaining ingredients.

* Buy unsulphured dried apricots in health food stores. They are drier in texture and dark in color, unlike those preserved with sulphur, and they taste much better — no metallic aftertaste.

Thai Cucumber Salad

Whether this crunchy cucumber dish is served as a salad or a condiment, it's a welcome addition to a plate of spicy Asian foods.

Use young European or Japanese cucumbers for this dish. They must be fresh and crisp and the seeds must be very small. Most of a cucumber's flavor is in its skin, so with this vegetable in particular, it pays to search out an organic source. Commercial cucumbers, whose skins have been waxed to prolong shelf-life, are totally unsuitable for this dish.

3½ cups finely diced organic cucumber, with skin

2 tablespoons lemon or lime juice

2 tablespoons ume plum vinegar

2 cloves pressed garlic

¼ teaspoon minced hot chile pepper (or to taste)

¼ cup minced Chinese parsley

Dice the cucumber and put it in a plastic container with a tight-fitting lid. Add the lemon, vinegar, garlic, and chile pepper; toss and refrigerate at least 30 minutes. Turn the container over a couple of times while it chills to be sure all the cucumbers receive the marinade.

Just before serving, drain the salad. Toss in the Chinese parsley and serve.

Yield: 6 servings

Variation:

Cilantro Tomatoes

To make cilantro tomatoes — a juicy and colorful accompaniment — substitute diced tomatoes for the cucumber in the preceding recipe. Also, increase the cilantro to ¼ cup.

Fruit Salad

Fruit lover that I am, it took me a long time to discover what makes a great fruit salad. Because I love fruit, all fruit salads tasted good — but some are better than good, and there's an art to making those particularly appealing ones.

For a great fruit salad you need a variety of ripe fruits in season, and the time and patience to cut your chosen fruits properly. For an extra-tempting salad, you might add a sauce, and to set it off, you'll want a beautiful serving bowl.

The right fruits are your personal favorites. Mine are mango, papaya, sweet pineapple, watermelon and seedless grapes. This is a fairly exotic combination, even here in Hawaii; the mango season is short, and the fruit is expensive. Ripe bananas are usually available, inexpensive, and do well in a fruit salad that is served on the day it's made.

When choosing fruits, consider the combination of colors and textures. Green or purple grapes, cream-colored bananas, orange papaya, red water-melon, and yellow pineapple make a stunning com-bination. The textural contrast is more subtle; all the fruits are relatively soft, yet the grapes offer some resistance to the bite, the watermelon is juicy, and the pineapple is chewy. I don't like anything firmer than pineapple in fruit salad; apples, for example, are too hard.

Other fruits that go well in salads include:
oranges
pink (or other sweet) grapefruit
tangerines
peeled pears
nectarines
apricots
peeled plums (unless you like the tart skin)
raisins
dried currants
dates
dried figs
fresh figs
persimmons
pomegranates
melons like cassaba, honeydew, and cantalope
kiwi fruit
passion fruit
raspberries
blackberries
blueberries
strawberries

Fruit-Cutting Guide

What makes eating fruit salad wonderful is the way the flavors and textures play together. This can only happen if the pieces of fruit are cut small enough so several can be taken in one bite. Remember this when you're chopping, and your salad will have that cared-for quality that makes it stand apart. Methods for tricky-to-cut fruits are described below.

Oranges and grapefruit: Peel the fruit deeply with a sharp knife, removing all of the white membrane as well as the skin. Then carefully cut the sections from the spokelike core. (With practice, you can leave the center membrane almost fruit-free.) Squeeze any juice left in the skin or the membrane into the salad. Chop the sections, removing any seeds.

Tangerines: Peel tangerines by hand, taking care to remove all the strings. Section the fruit, and cut the thick membrane from the center of each section; squeeze out the seeds. Chop the sections.

Pineapple: Cut off the top and about an inch of the fruit from the green end of the pineapple. (This is the sour end; you won't miss the fruit.) Cut the bottom off, too. With the pineapple standing firmly on the cut-off base, cut from top to bottom, removing the skin rather deeply (the point is to cut out all the "eyes"). Now cut it in half lengthwise; then in quarters. Remove the core from each quarter, and chop as desired.

Papaya: Cut the papaya in half lengthwise and carefully remove the seeds with a pointed spoon. Don't remove any of the flesh; there's precious little of it. Score the flesh in small squares with a dull knife (a butter knife is perfect); don't cut through the skin. Spoon out the small squares of papaya and discard the skin.

Kiwi fruit: Peel the thin skin from kiwi fruit closely with a sharp knife, then cut the fruit in rounds, half-rounds, or lengthwise quarters. Don't cut kiwi too finely or it will get lost in the salad.

Mango: The mango has a large, thin, almost flat seed that the trained eye can visualize within the fruit. It is situated between the mango's two "cheeks." Try to imagine the placement of the seed, and cut as closely to it as possible to liberate the cheeks. Once cut, score the flesh of each cheek into cubes with a small, sharp knife without cutting through the skin. Spoon the flesh from the skin. Peel the skin from the seed section, then cut off and chop the fruit.

Passion fruit: The passion fruit is full of sweet-tart, seedy, juicy pulp; there is no flesh. In fruit salad a bit of passion fruit is good, seeds and all.

Sauces for Fruit Salad

The best addition I know to fruit salad is Coconut Sauce, which is rich and creamy. For something lighter, try Strawberry Sauce. It's particularly good with pears, bananas, and oranges in a winter salad that needs a splash of color.

I've also included a Passion Fruit Sauce, in case you ever get your hands on more than a couple of these exotic fruits. This delectable trio of recipes can be found on page 140.

Salad Dressings

This is an important little section because it speaks to a simple subject few people address: making salad dressing. No need to expound upon the importance of a dressing. Like the envelope for a letter — it delivers.

There are a couple of excellent reasons to make your own salad dressing, and they both have to do with value. On a per-dollar basis, the cost of bottled salad dressings far exceeds the value of their ingredients and a reasonable surcharge for labor, packaging, and distribution. It's one of those high mark-up items worth avoiding. In addition, salad dressings are made with ingredients that vary greatly in quality. Even vigilant label-readers have no way to judge the quality of oils, vinegars, and condiments that bottled dressings contain.

If a person were to make just one change to upgrade his or her food program, making salad dressings wouldn't be a bad place to start. And once begun, it would invariably lead to eating more salads.

In my catering business, salad dressing recipes are among the most requested. After tasting the difference, people become willing, even eager, to re-create the unpurchaseable flavors at home.

Come to think of it, as far as pleasing people goes, making great dressings is the easiest way I know, short of becoming a pastry chef.

Olympian Dressing

Olympian dressing, based on Greek olives and extra-virgin olive oil, is my answer to the traditional Caesar Salad. While remarkably similar in taste, this dressing eliminates the fat and cholesterol of egg, Parmesan cheese, and anchovies.

½ cup extra-virgin olive oil

⅓ cup water (or, for extra flavor, juice from the olives, below)

½ cup fresh, firm tofu, mashed

1 tablespoon soy sauce

3 tablespoons lemon juice

2 cloves garlic, coarsely chopped

¼ cup pitted Kalamata olives (ripe black olives will not do)

Blenderize the first 5 ingredients until smooth. Then, with the blender running, add the garlic. After 30 seconds, with blender still running, and with your finger on the "off" button, add the olives. Blend just for a couple of seconds, until the olives are chopped, not puréed. Pour into a jar and chill thoroughly.

For New Caesar Salad, toss the dressing with chopped romaine, tomato wedges, and croutons. Use this dressing generously, to coat each leaf.

Yield: 6 to 8 servings (about 1⅔ cups)

A note: Dressings made with tofu tend to "set up" on standing, so by the second or third day you'll want to add a bit of water and shake or reblenderize them before serving.

Fresh Basil (or Parsley) Dressing

This bright green dressing reminds you of pesto with every bite. It has become a neighborhood favorite.

½ cup chopped onion

I small clove pressed garlic

½ teaspoon dry mustard

2 tablespoons honey (or to taste)

½ tablespoon white (or any light) miso

⅜ teaspoon salt (or to taste)

1¼ cups mild oil, such as canola

2 tablespoons extra-virgin olive oil

6 tablespoons water

¼ cup rice vinegar

2 tablespoons white wine vinegar

I cup fresh basil leaves (for Basil Dressing) or I teaspoon basil (as part of Parsley Dressing)

½ teaspoon oregano

¼ cup fresh parsley leaves

Blenderize all ingredients until thoroughly mixed. Season to taste, then chill and serve.

This dressing keeps very well, at least two weeks.

Yield: 12 to 16 servings (about 3 cups)

Cashew Lemon Dressing

This dressing has two distinctly different variations, one with dill and one with blue cheese. The Cashew Lemon Dill is reminiscent of buttermilk-based dressings that taste richer than they actually are. The Cashew Lemon Blue is both fresh and savory.

½ cup pure olive oil

¼ cup fresh lemon juice (with a bit of the zest, if the lemon is organic)

1½ teaspoons salt

I tablespoon mild honey

½ cup raw cashews

¾ cup water

I clove garlic

1½ teaspoons dill weed or 2 ounces blue cheese

For Cashew Lemon Dill: Place oil, lemon juice and zest, salt, honey, cashews, water, garlic, and dill in the blender. Blenderize until absolutely smooth, then transfer to a serving container or cruet and chill.

For Cashew Lemon Blue: Blenderize oil, lemon juice and zest, salt, honey, cashews, water, and garlic until absolutely smooth. Mash the blue cheese coarsely with a fork and stir it in to the dressing. Chill thoroughly before serving.

Yield: 8 servings (about 2 cups)

Toasted Sesame Dressing

In this dressing, which has both mild and bold variations, toasted sesame oil adds its own distinctive taste. I serve it atop raw greens as part of an unconventional Asian meal, or as a quick sauce for rice and vegetables.

3 tablespoons whole (unhulled) sesame seeds

⅓ cup mild oil, such as canola

1½ tablespoons toasted sesame oil

2 tablespoons rice vinegar

1 tablespoon mellow red miso

2 cloves garlic

¾ teaspoon salt

½ cup water

For a Mild Dressing: Blenderize everything until smooth. (It will take several minutes.)

For a Bold Dressing: Toast the sesame seeds 10 minutes at 300 degrees before blenderizing with the other ingredients. Substitute a dark miso, such as brown rice miso or barley miso, for the mellow red miso. Reduce water to ⅓ cup.

Proceed as for the mild version.

Yield: 4 servings (about 1 cup)

Honey-Mustard Vinaigrette

This dressing is a frequent resident in my refrigerator door. It can be made "mellow" or "strong" by including or omitting the soymilk. With soymilk, it's creamy and contains less fat and calories per serving. Without the soymilk, it's bold and refreshing.

¾ cup mild oil, such as canola

⅓ cup extra-virgin olive oil

¼ cup rice vinegar

1 tablespoon plus 2 teaspoons red wine vinegar

2 tablespoons honey

1 tablespoon Dijon mustard

1 to 2 cloves garlic, to taste

1 teaspoon salt

½ cup soymilk (optional)

Place all ingredients except soymilk in the blender and blend until smooth. For a mellow dressing, add the soymilk slowly with blender running; the dressing will thicken. Chill and serve.

Yield: 6 to 8 servings

Papaya Seed Dressing

If you buy papayas, save the seeds for this dressing. It's among the most-requested recipes at the seminars I cater, and it's simple to make. Papaya seeds are peppery in flavor, and there are about a thousand in a single fruit. (They sprout easily, too, if you'd like to start a papaya tree.)

¼ cup chopped onion
I large clove garlic
2 tablespoons Dijon mustard
3 tablespoons honey
I ½ teaspoons salt
¼ cup extra-virgin olive oil
¾ cup mild oil, such as canola
¼ cup rice vinegar
I tablespoon sherry wine vinegar
   (or balsamic vinegar)
½ teaspoon basil leaves
½ teaspoon oregano leaves
¼ cup water
2 tablespoons papaya seeds

Place all ingredients in blender and blend for about a minute, until dressing is well mixed and papaya seeds are partially broken down. They will appear as black flecks against a creamy background. Chill and serve.

Yield: 8 servings (about 2 cups)

Mediter-Asian Dressing

It must be the combination of three types of vinegar that gives this dressing its unusual, savory taste. It is one of my favorites, and it's quick to make.

Dressings made with nuts and seeds (or their butters) thicken on standing. They may be thinned with a bit of water, or by reblending.

½ cup mild oil, such as canola
¼ cup extra-virgin olive oil
3 tablespoons rice vinegar
2 tablespoons balsamic vinegar
⅓ cup cashew nut butter or ½ cup
   raw cashews
2 tablespoons honey
½ cup water
I tablespoon ume plum vinegar
I tablespoon soy sauce
I ½ teaspoons Dijon mustard
I teaspoon dried basil leaves
I large clove garlic

Place all ingredients in blender and blenderize until creamy and smooth, about 3 minutes. Chill and serve.

Yield: 6 to 8 servings (about 1¾ cups)

Garden Goddess

Creamy, thick, and rich with garden-fresh parsley, my taste buds hail this as the ultimate low-fat dressing.

1 cup chopped parsley
Half a small zucchini, coarsely
    chopped
¼ pound fresh tofu
⅓ cup extra-virgin olive oil
2 tablespoons raw tahini
1 tablespoon soy sauce
1 teaspoon seasoned salt
1 teaspoon dried basil leaf
1 clove garlic
3 tablespoons lemon juice
⅔ cup water

Put everything in the blender and blend for several minutes, until smooth; chill and serve. Keeps one week, refrigerated. Reblend it in the blender with a bit of water if you're serving it a few days after making.

Yield: 8 to 10 servings (more than 2 cups)

Green Tahini Dressing

The vegetables in this dressing give it a fresh, clean flavor, while the oils and tahini provide richness in the background. The combination is especially appealing over a variety of greens, including bitters such as arugula, mustard leaves, and young kale. Green Tahini Dressing definitely improves with age, even an hour, so try to prepare it well before mealtime.

¼ cup raw tahini
¼ cup lemon juice
¼ cup mild oil, such as canola
¼ cup extra-virgin olive oil
¼ cup chopped onion
½ cup chopped green pepper
1 stalk chopped celery (optional)
2 tablespoons chopped parsley
1 teaspoon salt
1 teaspoon honey

Blenderize all ingredients until absolutely smooth. Chill, shake, and serve.

Yield: 6 to 8 servings (about 1½ cups)

Dips & Condiments

Homemade dips and condiments are the non-essentials of a meal — the culinary flourishes that embellish it, that lift it from the ordinary with bursts of intense flavor, creamy smoothness, or brilliance of hue. They're like savory little desserts that couldn't wait. Because they are non-essential, even frivolous, these silent items say without a word that something special is going on, that special care has been taken for some reason, or for no reason at all.

I want a dip to tantalize, not satisfy me, so I can take my hunger to the table rather than leave it at the hors d'oeuvre tray. Since it is fat that fills us the fastest, dips shouldn't contain too much of it; you won't find any cream cheese or sour cream dips here.

Condiments are like kites; they can't fly on their own. But given a solid base, they can soar above the crowd. The Pennsylvania Dutch made an art of embellishing their meals with tasty condiments — seven sweets and seven sours. Indonesian cuisine does the same, with small bowls of raisins, peanuts, coconut, green onions, as well as various pickles and sambals (highly spiced relishes). Whatever the number, the purpose of condiments is to enhance, not to overpower, and for this reason they are served in garnish-sized portions.

Even the most basic of condiments can make a difference. If dinner is plain, consider adding a tray with small bowls of chopped Chinese parsley, toasted almonds, marinated artichoke hearts, cherry tomatoes, or fresh tofu sprinkled with tamari, ginger, and green onions. Without much work, a full condiment tray can turn a simple bowl of rice into a feast.

Avocado Dip

Avocado is a marvelous fruit, and one we almost always have in the house. Avo trees produce year-round where we live, so avocados are abundant and reasonably priced. Although we've cut back on fat in other areas, I haven't found it necessary to reduce our avocado intake. They seem easy to digest and easy on the waistline despite their fat content.

I've tasted a host of avocado concoctions and versions of guacamole. My complaint with most is that they're full of strong-tasting ingredients like tomatoes, lemon, onion, and Chinese parsley. Personally, I love the flavor of avocado itself, and the dip I prefer plays solely on that one grand taste.

We use this for dipping vegetable spears and corn chips, and also as a topping for baked potatoes, green salads, steamed vegetables, and rice. It's also good instead of butter under a slice of cheese on sourdough toast.

2 cups mashed avocado
1½ teaspoons soy sauce
½ teaspoon seasoned salt
⅛ teaspoon salt (or to taste)
1 large clove pressed garlic

Combine all ingredients thoroughly and serve immediately. Store with plastic wrap pressed against the surface. If protected this way and refrigerated, avocado will hold its color for a couple of days. But there's no substitute for fresh Avo Dip served at room temperature.

Yield: 4 to 6 servings (about 2 cups)

It's considered lucky to have geckos in your house because they eat the critters we like least. Even a giant cockroach is no match for the wily lizards; and to a gecko, mosquitos are like "fast foods." But my favorite gecko trait is the chirping, chuckling sound they make. It never fails to amaze me how they chuckle at the most appropriate moments.

Azuki Bean Dip

Aduki, Azuki, Adzuki: However you spell it (all are correct), this small red bean is highly prized by the macrobiotic food community for its sweet flavor, which indicates a perfect yin/yang (alkaline/acid) balance.

I've always wanted to celebrate azuki beans for this reason, but it's been tough going. They are not what you'd call user-friendly beans. In numerous experiments I've found them dry and boring, even after long cooking with kombu (seaweed), as macrobiotic cookbooks suggest. And while pressure cooking does succeed in softening them, it also destroys their character.

Azukis do sprout easily, though, and make a refreshing, crunchy salad vegetable. For a long time, I thought that was the best I could do with them. Then I tried a recipe for an azuki bean dip in The Natural Gourmet by Annemarie Colbin. She purées the beans with water and a few other ingredients (including umeboshi paste), and creates a most unusual and delicious dip. I, too, decided to blenderize the tough little buggers. What a difference a blade makes — they become surprisingly creamy and smooth.

2 cups well-cooked azuki beans (pressure cooking is the most efficient cooking method; it takes 20 minutes even for unsoaked beans)

1 tablespoon extra-virgin olive oil

4 tablespoons bean cooking water

1 tablespoon soy sauce

2 small cloves garlic

1 teaspoon chili powder

scant ¼ teaspoon salt

3 tablespoons minced sweet onion

3 tablespoons diced roasted chiles (canned are fine)

Blenderize beans, oil, 2 tablespoons cooking water, soy sauce, garlic, chili powder, and salt. When absolutely smooth, scrape the dip into a serving bowl and add the onion, chiles, and remaining bean water to desired consistency. Serve with corn chips.

Yield: 4 to 6 servings (about 2 cups)

Hummus Two Ways

Hummus is a creamy Lebanese dip, traditionally made with garbanzo beans, sesame tahini, garlic, and lemon. I ordered it in a small vegetarian café in London without knowing exactly what it was. That was in 1972 but I still remember the intrigue of the first bite: unusual, exotic, delicious.

The creamiest hummus is made in the blender rather than the food processor. Just remember making it in the blender takes your full attention, frequent stops, and a willingness to help the blender considerably with a rubber spatula.

I've included two versions of hummus here — my old, faithful recipe (more beany, and rich-tasting), and a new lighter-tasting variation. Serve hummus with pita bread wedges or the small, inner leaves of romaine lettuce for dipping.

For Recipe 1:

2 cups well-cooked garbanzo beans (unsalted)

1 large clove garlic

1 teaspoon salt

2 tablespoons lemon juice

¼ cup raw tahini

½ to ⅔ cup water (or bean cooking water)

For Recipe 2:

1 box firm, silken tofu

1 cup cooked garbanzo beans

⅔ cup raw tahini

⅓ cup lemon juice (or more to taste)

2 cloves garlic

1½ teaspoons salt (or to taste)

Place all ingredients in the blender. (For Recipe 1, the traditional version, start with the smallest amount of water.) Pulse the blender several times to get it going. Once it has started, select a low speed and blend it, increasing the speed until the blender motor sounds strained. Stop the machine, and use a rubber spatula to push chunky portions of the mixture into the blades. Continue blending, stopping, and pushing the mixture into the blades as necessary until the hummus is totally smooth, adding water if necessary.

Taste and season as desired. Some people add a dash of cayenne, others add cumin. Increase the tahini, garlic, salt, or lemon if you prefer stronger flavors; taste and see. I don't add spices (or even too much lemon) because the simple richness of the tahini-bean combination is fantastic as it is.

Yield: Recipe 1: 4 to 6 servings (about 2 cups)
Recipe 2: 8 to 12 servings (about 3½ cups)

Sesame-Vegetable Mélange

This mélange, or mixture, makes a creamy and delectable dip, especially when served with crisp crackers like lavosh (Armenian bread).

1 pound eggplant (1 large)
1 teaspoon olive oil
¼ cup raw tahini
6 tablespoons water
2 cloves garlic
3 tablespoons lemon juice
½ teaspoon salt
1 tomato
1 tablespoon sesame seeds
1 tablespoon minced parsley

Cut the eggplant in half lengthwise and place it on a small baking sheet greased with the olive oil. Set the oven to 400 degrees and bake the eggplant until the skin is crisp and the pulp is very soft, about 45 minutes. At the same time, toast the sesame seeds in the oven in a small pan. Watch them carefully so they don't burn. The oven is really too hot for sesame seeds, but if you bake them only 8 minutes, starting in a cold oven, they'll be fine (set your timer).

When the eggplant is done and cool enough to handle, scoop the pulp of one half into the blender container. Add the tahini, water, garlic, lemon juice, and salt; blend until smooth and put the mixture in a bowl.

Peel the remaining eggplant half and chop the pulp finely. Add it to the bowl. Cut the tomato in half across the width, and squeeze it firmly (over the sink) to remove the seeds; chop the tomato and add it to the bowl. Mix well and place the dip in a serving bowl.

Combine the minced parsley and toasted sesame seeds. Sprinkle them over the dip and serve at room temperature.

Yield: 6 to 8 servings

Banana Chutney

Complex in flavor yet simple to make, this condiment adds an exotic touch to any Indonesian or Indian meal. Its sweetness complements the spicy, hot, and sour flavors on the plate. Although chutneys do keep well, I prefer to eat this one within a few days of making it, while the bananas are still fresh and firm.

½ cup seedless raisins
½ cup pitted, chopped dates
¼ cup honey
¼ cup barley malt vinegar
   (or rice vinegar)
¼ cup water
2 teaspoons brown mustard seed
½ teaspoon ginger powder
½ teaspoon salt
¼ teaspoon cayenne
1½ cups peeled, chopped banana
   (about 2 medium)

In a saucepan over medium heat, cook the raisins, dates, honey, vinegar, water, and spices, mixing well. When the mixture boils, reduce the heat and cover. Simmer 10 minutes, then add the chopped banana. Cook uncovered 5 minutes more, then remove it from the pot to cool. Chill and serve.

Yield: 6 servings (more than 2 cups)

Red Onion Raita

Raita, or chilled yogurt sauce, is a common Indian condiment. It offers contrast of taste, temperature, and texture when served alongside hot curries. The most common raitas include a vegetable — usually cucumber — to add a bit of crunch and extra coolness.

This raita plays upon the pungent sweetness of red onion in combination with cucumber, tomato, and yogurt. Freshly roasted cumin, salt, and cilantro leaves add the finishing touch.

1 teaspoon cumin seeds
2 cups plain yogurt
1 small red onion, minced
   (about ½ cup)
1 tomato, seeded and finely
   chopped
Half a cucumber, peeled, seeded
   and coarsely grated
½ teaspoon salt
1 tablespoon Chinese parsley,
   finely chopped

No question about it, freshly roasted and ground cumin seeds taste far better than pre-ground cumin. It's easy to roast and grind the seeds; dry fry them in a skillet over medium heat for a minute or two, then grind them with a mortar and pestle.

Combine the yogurt, vegetables, and seasonings; chill and serve.

Yield: 4 to 6 servings (about 3 cups)

Sauces

The tongue has a memory for good sauces. Mine recalls with pleasure its first Black Bean Sauce and its first Passion Fruit Sauce. It draws me like a magnet to a restaurant where I once tasted pasta with a sauce I can't forget, yet can't describe. Unlike classic, savory sauces, which are based upon the drippings of meat, fowl, or fish, vegetarian sauces gain their flavor largely from plant sources such as soy sauce, miso, peanut butter, fermented black beans, mushrooms, and tomatoes. Familiarity with these ingredients and a few sauce-making techniques can turn an ordinary cook into a creative and satisfied chef de cuisine.

Tahini-Miso A Sauce for All Seasons

One of the questions I like to ask when I'm interviewing a chef for a magazine article is this, "What do you fix to eat when you're home alone?" If I were asked, the answer would be this sauce. Whether I'm having salad, steamed vegetables, pasta, or a sandwich, this is the sauce I choose to top it off. It's simple to make, but the flavor is always interesting because of the miso in the base.

½ cup raw tahini

3 to 4 tablespoons mellow red miso

6 tablespoons water (more or less, to desired taste and texture)

1 clove pressed garlic (optional)

For a thinner liquid dressing, whisk all the ingredients together in a small bowl. For a thicker spread, use less water, and mash the ingredients together with a wooden spoon until they are thoroughly blended.

It doesn't get much easier than this.

Yield: 3 to 4 servings (about 1 cup)

Peanut Sauce

This uncooked sauce is whisked together in a matter of minutes, and makes a fabulous topping for a wide variety of foods, especially vegetables. Try it over raw vegetable salads, particularly those made with cabbage.

Don't toss Peanut Sauce into your salads or stir-fries; instead, serve it on the side. This prevents the sauce from drawing liquid from the vegetables.

⅓ cup peanut butter

⅓ cup mild oil, such as canola

3½ tablespoons soy sauce

2 tablespoons plus 2 teaspoons honey

1 tablespoon plus 2 teaspoons white wine vinegar

1½ teaspoons toasted sesame oil

½ teaspoon salt

⅛ teaspoon cayenne

Whisk the peanut butter and oil together; when the mixture is smooth, whisk in the remaining ingredients.

Yield: 3 servings (about 1 cup)

Béchamel Nouvelle

Béchamel, or "white sauce," isn't white in this recipe. It's golden brown from roasted whole wheat flour, and it tastes mildly rich and earthy. I like its mellow flavor over strong-tasting greens like kale, spinach, and chard.

2 tablespoons olive oil
2 tablespoons whole wheat flour
2 tablespoons soy sauce
1 to 1½ cups soymilk or milk
Salt and pepper (optional)

Heat the oil in a saucepan until it's hot, then whisk in the flour. Keep whisking for about 2 minutes, over medium heat, then add the soy sauce and 1 cup of the milk gradually, whisking all the time. Bring the sauce to a simmer.

Continue to simmer the sauce for about 10 minutes, whisking frequently. As it thickens, whisk in additional milk to your chosen consistency. Season to taste with salt and pepper.

Yield: 3 to 4 servings (about 1½ cups)

VARIATIONS:

Herbed Béchamel

Use the béchamel as a base when experimenting with herbs. By adding ¼ to ½ teaspoon, you'll find it easy to single out and identify the flavor of tarragon, cumin, or any herb you try. Add the herb to the hot oil, at the beginning.

Garbanzo Béchamel

Use garbanzo bean flour instead of whole wheat flour. It imparts a rich, nutty flavor.

Béchamel de Beurre

Use butter instead of olive oil.

Other Options

Sauté something flavorful like minced onion or garlic in the oil, or add something fresh and colorful like minced Italian parsley to the finished sauce.

Spaghetti Sauce

People love spaghetti, especially when it's served with an easy to make, long-simmered sauce like this one. Add a crisp green salad and pass a bowl of freshly-grated hard cheese. Parmesan is always good, but so are Asiago, Fontinella, and Kasseri.

⅓ cup olive oil

2 small onions, chopped

2 large cloves pressed garlic

1 small, round eggplant, finely diced

¼ teaspoon salt

1 28-ounce can Italian plum tomatoes (or peeled, chopped tomatoes)

1 14-ounce can Italian plum tomatoes (or peeled, chopped tomatoes)

1 green pepper, chopped

1 bay leaf

3 ounces tomato paste

¼ cup chopped parsley

½ teaspoon basil leaf

½ teaspoon oregano leaf

Red wine (optional)

Salt to taste

Heat the olive oil and sauté the onions, garlic, and eggplant until tender, about 12 minutes. Mix in the ¼ teaspoon salt and add the two cans of tomatoes. (If they're whole, chop or squeeze, to break them down.) Also add the pepper and the bay leaf. Bring the pot to a boil, then add the tomato paste. Mix it until it dissolves, and when the pot boils again, reduce the heat to a simmer.

At this point, you can let the sauce simmer, uncovered, for hours, adding red wine as the liquid evaporates, and stirring often. The longer it cooks, the richer the sauce becomes, but if you don't have hours, 30 minutes is enough.

10 minutes before serving, add the parsley, basil, oregano, and a maximum of 2 tablespoons red wine. (More wine than that doesn't have time to "burn off.")

Remove the bay leaf. Season the sauce to taste with salt. Serve over one pound of freshly cooked spaghetti.

Yield: 4 to 6 servings (about 7 cups)

Indonesian Sauce

Rich, creamy, and exotic, this sauce can turn an ordinary wokful of vegetables into quick party fare. It's particularly good with stir-fried broccoli, sweet red peppers, and hot-but-still-crisp cabbage. Sprinkle chopped peanuts over all for extra crunch.

¼ **cup soy sauce**
¼ **cup water**
¼ **cup honey**
3 to 4 tablespoons rice vinegar (to taste)
¼ **cup smooth peanut butter**
½ **cup coconut milk**
⅛ **to ¼ teaspoon cayenne (optional)**
1½ **tablespoons cornstarch or 2 tablespoons kuzu**
1½ **tablespoons water**

Whisk together or blenderize the soy sauce, the ¼ cup water, honey, vinegar, peanut butter, coconut milk, and cayenne, if you like it spicy. Pour it into a saucepan.

Dissolve the thickener in the 1½ tablespoons water, mix it well, and add it to the saucepan. Heat the sauce gently, whisking often, until it's thick.

Yield: about 6 servings (almost 2 cups)

Ten-Minute Mushroom Stroganoff

For a rich and succulent topping for pasta, grains, or vegetables, this is a quick and easy sauce. The taste of tofu disappears and the chewy mushroom chunks take the limelight.

1 pound mushrooms (large, with open gills, preferably)
4 tablespoons butter
¼ **cup soy sauce**
2 cloves garlic
2 packages firm, silken tofu

Clean the mushrooms and slice them thickly. Sauté them in butter in a large, shallow pot until they begin to release liquid.

While the mushrooms are cooking, put the soy sauce, the garlic, and the silken tofu in the blender; blenderize until absolutely smooth.

Add the blender mixture to the mushrooms in the pot and heat through. That's it!

Yield: 4 servings (about 4 cups)

Chinese Brown Sauce

A *magic recipe if ever there were one, this quick and simple soy-based sauce transforms whatever it touches. The taste is fresh and unassuming; there's not a vegetable that wouldn't be happy to wear it.*

How to use it? Let me count three ways:

Top steaming rice, grilled tofu cubes, and any stir-fried vegetable with Chinese Brown Sauce and a sprinkling of toasted cashews.

Serve Chinese Brown Sauce over Tofu Patties (page 118).

Serve Chinese Brown Sauce with sautéed tempeh over buckwheat noodles, steamed pumpkin, red pepper, and broccoli. Sprinkle toasted almonds on top.

2 teaspoons mild oil, such as canola

½ cup minced onion

I clove pressed garlic

I teaspoon peeled and finely grated ginger

I cup water

¼ cup soy sauce

¼ cup cold water in which I tablespoon cornstarch (or 1½ tablespoons kuzu) has been dissolved

I teaspoon toasted sesame oil

Heat the oil over medium heat in a saucepan, and fry the minced onion until it is transparent, about 3 minutes. Add the garlic and ginger and continue to fry for 3 to 5 minutes, or until the onion begins to brown. Add the water and soy sauce, and bring to a simmer. Add the dissolved thickener and whisk the sauce until it thickens. Add the sesame oil, and it's ready to serve.

Yield: 6 servings (about 1½ cups)

Tofu "Mayonnaise" or "Sour Cream"

The creamy texture of blenderized tofu lends itself to the creation of smooth sauces like mayonnaise and sour cream. The tofu-based versions have distinct nutritional advantages because they're higher in protein, lower in fat, and contain no cholesterol.

In the arena of flavor, tofu sour cream and tofu mayonnaise are surprisingly suitable for most purposes. Only in sandwich-making is tofu mayonnaise inappropriate since it tends to make the bread soggy.

The taste of the tofu mayo or tofu sour cream you create depends on the flavor of the tofu itself, so experiment with various brands to find one you like best. For variety, add your preferred tastes, such as lemon or lime juice, mustard, horseradish, or ginger, to the ingredients below.

½ cup firm tofu (may be silken)
2 tablespoons nutritional yeast (optional)
2 tablespoons water (if necessary for blending)
1 tablespoon soy sauce
1 tablespoon extra-virgin olive oil

Place all ingredients in the blender and blenderize until absolutely smooth. Stop several times during blending to guide the mixture into the blades when necessary.

Yield: 3 servings (about ¾ cup)

Salsa

Salsa is a staple at our house. We keep it on hand for use on tortillas, to garnish rice and beans, and as a tasty topping for soups and baked potatoes.

This is the salsa I make most frequently because it teams two important elements: freshness and convenience. It's based on Ortega brand Green Chile Salsa, with fresh tomatoes, sweet onion, and Chinese parsley added.

1 7-ounce can green chile salsa
1 cup finely chopped fresh tomato
⅓ cup chopped sweet onion
2 small cloves pressed garlic
Minced hot chile peppers (or cayenne powder) to taste
2 tablespoons minced Chinese parsley
Salt if desired

Combine all ingredients, and season to taste with hot chiles or cayenne, and salt.

Yield: 6 to 8 servings (2 cups)

Basil Pesto and Cilantro Pesto

A *pesto is an intense, concentrated Italian sauce. The most well-known pesto is made of basil leaves ground with olive oil, Parmesan cheese, garlic and pine nuts. It is one of the deepest, richest flavors ever to cross the tongue. As such, it's the perfect complement to pasta.*

Could anything be as good as basil pesto, I wondered? I decided to try making it with Chinese parsley instead of basil. The results were surprising.

Basil pesto has a dark, intense, seductive flavor. It grabs your attention and keeps it. Cilantro pesto, on the other hand, charms you like a spring morning.

For the Basil Pesto:

½ cup extra-virgin olive oil
2 cloves garlic
4 cups fresh basil leaves, packed
½ cup grated Parmesan
½ cup pine nuts or walnuts
Salt to taste

For the Cilantro Pesto:

½ cup olive oil
2 cloves garlic
4 cups Chinese parsley, packed
⅓ cup grated Parmesan
¼ cup pine nuts or walnuts
Salt to taste
1½ cups additional Chinese parsley, packed (to be blended in after the first leaves are blended smooth)

Making pesto is a cooperative effort between you and your blender. Your job is to keep feeding the pesto ingredients into the blender blades, while keeping your rubber spatula out of them.

Place all ingredients in the blender container in the order listed. Blend, slowly at first, then faster as the blades catch the leaves. Stop as frequently as necessary to reposition the mixture around the blades; blend until a smooth paste is formed. This takes patience, but after you've made pesto a couple of times, it becomes easy.

We use pesto in several ways. The most straightforward is to toss it directly into hot pasta and mix like crazy (it's thick). Instead, I usually heat the pesto in a large pot or wok and dilute it with soymilk or milk to the consistency of a thick batter. This thins the pesto, so it's easy to mix with the hot pasta.

Pesto is also fantastic combined with an equal amount of mayonnaise, spread on baguettes, and broiled until bubbly.

It's also great on cheese and tomato sandwiches, in guacamole, and mounded atop baked or mashed potatoes.

Yield: 4 to 6 servings (enough for 1 pound of pasta)

Green Chile Pesto

I first tasted Green Chile Pesto on a fabulous veggie burger at Maui Coffee Roasters in Kahului. Owner Nick Matichyn uses macadamia nuts in his pesto; I've substituted pine nuts because they're more widely available. The concept of chiles in pesto was totally foreign to me until the moment it kissed my lips. What a taste!

7 ounces (about 1 cup) canned green chiles, chopped

2 cloves garlic

1 cup Chinese parsley or basil leaves, packed into measuring cup

½ cup pine nuts (or chopped macadamia nuts)

¼ cup extra-virgin olive oil

1 teaspoon salt

Blenderize everything using the pulse feature on the blender. Don't aim for a totally smooth paste; it's good to retain some of the texture of the nuts.

This pesto is great on sandwiches and as a topping for pasta, steamed vegetables, grains, and baked potatoes.

Yield: 3 to 4 servings (more than 1½ cups or enough to top 8 oz. of pasta)

Black Bean Sauce

To assure using the right beans for this recipe, please read about black beans in the Glossary before preparing this recipe.

Black Bean Sauce is excellent over stir-fried vegetables and rice.

1 tablespoon kuzu or cornstarch

1 tablespoon soy sauce

1 tablespoon sherry

2 tablespoons Chinese black beans, rinsed and minced

¾ cup vegetable bouillon

1 tablespoon mild oil, such as canola

2 large cloves pressed garlic

1 teaspoon finely grated ginger

Dash white pepper

Combine cornstarch (or kuzu), soy sauce and sherry; set aside.

Rinse and mince the black beans; prepare the vegetable bouillon and reserve it. Heat the oil and sauté the garlic and ginger for 1 minute, then add the black beans and sauté an additional minute. Add the hot bouillon and a dash of white pepper; bring the sauce to a boil, then add the reserved thickener mixture and simmer until the sauce thickens, about 1 minute.

Yield: 3 to 4 servings (about 1 cup)

Hot Pasta

Since my first taste of Kraft's Macaroni and Cheese, I've been hooked on pasta. My mother also made something called Macaroni and Egg (elbow macaroni tossed with salt, pepper, and beaten eggs, fried in lots of butter), which I would have eaten every night with complete satisfaction — and still could. And because there are so many shapes, varieties, and combinations, pasta is always interesting, even if we eat it twice a week.

Cooking pasta is simple. First, use plenty of water — at least three times as much as would be necessary to cover it. *Joy of Cooking* recommends using seven quarts of boiling water and one tablespoon each of salt and olive oil per pound of pasta. Using this much water allows it to become hot enough to remain boiling when the pasta is added, ensuring rapid and thorough cooking.

Select a pasta shape appropriate to the sauce you'll use. For example, long shapes like fettucini and linguini are particularly well-suited to pesto, which coats the long strands. Chunky tomato-vegetable sauces are more appropriate with chunky pastas like rigatoni, so the eater finds both pasta and veggies at the end of her fork. Cheesy sauces are good on all shapes.

Two last words about pasta: al dente. You probably know the Italian expression, which means "to the tooth," and refers to what Italians consider the perfect degree of doneness. While it's true that pasta should not be overcooked, it's equally true that it must not be underdone. I check pasta for doneness repeatedly while it cooks, grabbing a slippery strand from the pot as best I can and biting into it. My taste is for greater doneness than the time given on the package, so I cook it to my taste. I'm sure that's what al dente ultimately means.

Pasta Perfecta

Right now, this is my favorite recipe in the book. I just ate it for lunch. As you scan the ingredients, you'll notice some expensive ones — dried tomatoes, pine nuts, basil, fresh Parmesan cheese. But the amounts are small, and the flavor rewards are immense. I'd be completely satisfied to receive this dish in the finest Italian restaurant. (In fact, I'd go especially for it.) Compared to restaurant prices, making this at home is a real bargain. And it's ready in 20 minutes.

½ **pound linguini**
2 **teaspoons salt**
2 **tablespoons extra-virgin olive oil**
5 **cloves pressed garlic**
½ **cup boiling water**
7 **dried tomato halves**
2 **tablespoons Chinese black beans
   (see Glossary)**
½ **cup chopped basil leaves**
1 **tablespoon water**
1 **tablespoon extra-virgin olive oil**
3 **tablespoons pine nuts**
2 **to 4 tablespoons freshly grated
   Parmesan cheese**

Bring a large pot of water to boil and add the 2 teaspoons of salt. When the water boils, add the linguini. When the water returns to a boil, set the timer for 12 minutes.

While you're waiting for the water to boil, heat the 2 tablespoons of oil in a skillet. Add the garlic and cook it over very low heat.

Pour the ½ cup boiling water over the tomato halves in a small bowl. Rinse and mince the Chinese black beans, and add them to the garlic in the skillet. Let them simmer while you chop the basil.

When the tomatoes have softened, add their soaking water to the skillet. Chop the tomatoes, and add them when the water in the skillet boils. Increase heat to medium and simmer 5 minutes.

Add the basil, and the 1 tablespoon each of water and oil. When it boils, reduce the heat and add the pine nuts.

By now, the pasta should be done. Drain it thoroughly, shaking the colander until all the water is gone. Place the pasta on individual plates and top it with the sauce and Parmesan cheese. (It won't look like enough sauce, but it is. The flavor is strong.)

Yield: 2 lunch servings, or 4 first-course servings

Originally, when we built the kitchen, we placed it on the wrong (west) side of the house. In summertime, the afternoon sun would turn my favorite room into a sauna. So we planted a fast-growing type of bamboo outside the window, and soon it was higher than the roof. The bamboo provides some shade, some screening, and a gentle rustle that sounds a lot like rain. The bamboo patch is also home to a few twittering families of Japanese "white-eyes" (the tiny yellow-green bird, mejiro). Such are the fruits of our error.

Pastitsio

For the sheer joy of eating, this is one of my favorite dishes. If there's anything more comforting (or more delicious) than pasta with two sauces, feta cheese, and butter, I've yet to taste it. And, Pastitsio is surprisingly quick and easy to make.

This recipe is noteworthy because each of the three parts — the tomato sauce, the béchamel sauce, and the pasta itself — contains wonderful flavors of its own. I've eaten the pasta without the sauces, and I've used the sauces over a variety of bases; any way you put it together, this recipe yields outstanding results.

For the Pasta:

3 cups (½ pound plus ½ cup) penne (tubular pasta with angled ends)
¼ cup butter, coarsely chopped
½ cup feta cheese, finely cubed

For the Tomato Sauce:

1 pound canned tomatoes, with juice
8 to 10 cloves pressed garlic (or to taste)
3 tablespoons olive oil
2 tablespoons fresh basil (or 1 teaspoon dried basil leaves)
½ teaspoon salt (or to taste)

For the Béchamel:

1⅓ cups milk
4 tablespoons whole wheat pastry flour
⅓ cup cream cheese
Salt and pepper to taste

For the Garnish:

Fresh basil sprigs or 2 tablespoons minced parsley

Bring 3 quarts of water to a boil for the penne. Add 2 rounded teaspoons salt. Cook the pasta until almost al dente (slightly underdone); it will cook more in the oven. Drain the cooked pasta thoroughly and mix it with the butter and feta cheese. Try to restrain yourself from eating it as is, and set it aside.

For the tomato sauce, blenderize all the ingredients until smooth.

For the béchamel, heat half the milk gently in a small saucepan; blenderize the other half with the flour, and add it when the milk in the saucepan is warm. Also add the cream cheese. Whisk the sauce regularly as it heats and keep a sharp eye on it so it doesn't burn or boil over. When it begins to boil, reduce the heat to a simmer, and cook it for 5 minutes. Season to taste with salt and pepper.

To assemble, butter an attractive baking dish, preferably a round one that is at least 2½ inches deep. Layer half the béchamel, half the pasta, and half the tomato sauce. Repeat the layers and bake uncovered 35 minutes at 400 degrees. Garnish and serve.

Yield: 4 to 5 servings

Penne with Broccoli, Mushrooms, and Walnut Sauce

The creamy Walnut Sauce that makes this dish so good is simple to prepare. Toss it with penne, broccoli, sautéed mushrooms, and toasted walnut bits for an elegant entrée.

For the Walnut Sauce:

1 piece whole wheat bread, crusts removed

¾ cup soymilk or milk

¾ cup walnuts

1 clove garlic

2 tablespoons olive oil

½ cup freshly grated Asiago or Parmesan cheese

¾ teaspoon salt

For the Rest:

12 ounces penne

3 cups broccoli florets

¾ pound mushrooms (preferably mature, with gills open)

2 tablespoons butter

2 tablespoons soy sauce

½ cup chopped walnuts

¼ cup minced Italian parsley

Before starting the sauce, toast the ½ cup walnuts in the oven for 8 to 10 minutes at 300 degrees; reserve.

To make the sauce, soak the bread in the soymilk. Place nuts, garlic, oil, cheese, salt, and the bread-milk mixture in the blender, and blend until smooth, about 3 minutes. Reserve.

Cook the penne in plenty of boiling, salted water, and steam the broccoli lightly (until tender, but still bright green). Sauté the mushrooms in butter; just before they're done, add the soy sauce. When the soy sauce boils, toss in the steamed broccoli and mix well. Leave the vegetables partially uncovered to preserve the broccoli's color.

Drain the pasta and toss it with the vegetables, the sauce, half the parsley, and half the toasted walnuts. Place in a serving dish and garnish with the remaining parsley and toasted walnuts.

Yield: 4 to 6 servings

SUGGESTED MENU
Penne with Broccoli, Mushrooms, and Walnut Sauce
Green Salad with Arugula and Honey-Mustard Dressing
Corn Squares Supreme
Pumpkin Pie

Macajiki and Cheese

Combining hijiki, macaroni, and Parmesan cheese seemed unusual the first time I tried it, but the casserole was well-received (devoured, actually), so I made it again. The result was the same.

This is a great dish for novice sea-vegetable eaters, or novice tofu eaters, for that matter. The macaroni-cheesy flavor is predominant, which seems to be what counts.

½ pound elbow macaroni
½ cup hijiki
2 teaspoons salt
½ cup chopped onion
3 cloves pressed garlic
1 tablespoon mild oil
1 cup chopped carrots
1 bell pepper (red or green),
  finely chopped
½ pound firm tofu, finely cubed
  (optional)
3 tablespoons soy sauce
¾ cup soymilk or milk
¾ cup Parmesan cheese
½ cup minced Italian parsley

Rinse the hijiki thoroughly, then cook it with the pasta and salt in abundant boiling water. While it cooks, sauté the onion in the oil; after 3 minutes, add the garlic and carrots; 3 minutes later, add the pepper and tofu. Sprinkle soy sauce over the tofu and vegetables and cook until done to taste. When the pasta is ready, drain it thoroughly. Add the vegetable mixture, the soymilk, the Parmesan, and the parsley. Mix well and serve. If made ahead, the dish can be reheated in the oven, covered, for 20 to 25 minutes at 325 degrees.

Yield: 4 servings

Feta-Noodle Kugel

Kugel can best be described as a savory noodle pudding, kind of a cross between macaroni and cheese and quiche. My grandmother's (which I've adapted here) was the world's best.

8 ounces ribbon noodles

4 beaten eggs

I cup crumbled feta cheese

⅔ cup cottage cheese

⅔ cup sour cream or tofu sour cream (page 67)

3 tablespoons melted butter (more, if you like)

¾ teaspoon salt

½ teaspoon seasoned salt

⅓ cup minced onion

I tablespoon soymilk or milk

Bring 3½ quarts of water to boil; boil noodles gently until they are barely done, then drain them. Shake the strainer or colander vigorously to remove all the water. Preheat the oven to 375 degrees.

While the noodles boil, combine the beaten eggs, feta, cottage cheese, sour cream, melted butter, salt, seasoned salt, and minced onion in a large mixing bowl. Add the drained noodles and mix gently but thoroughly.

Transfer the noodle mixture to a buttered 9-inch square casserole; distribute the noodles evenly. Pour the milk into a tablespoon and drag the spoon over the kugel, releasing the milk slowly over the entire surface. Bake until set and golden, about 60 minutes. Let rest for 5 minutes, then serve.

Yield: 4 to 6 servings

Buckwheat Noodles
with Vegetables and Kasseri Cheese

This is one of the easiest preparations in the book, even though it includes another entire recipe. The simple technique of adding vegetables to a pot of bubbling pasta just before the pasta is done makes this dish fresh and fast. The vegetables are quickly cooked, they retain their bright color and crunch, and no extra pots need to be washed. The additional recipe, Irresistible Mushrooms, can be put together while the pasta is cooking. You can make it before, during, or after the pasta and vegetables are done.

2 teaspoons salt

12 ounces buckwheat noodles
   (soba)

6 cups chopped vegetables
   (a combination of chopped
   broccoli, sweet red pepper, and
   small, sliced zucchini is good)

3 tablespoons extra-virgin olive oil

1 tablespoon ume plum vinegar

1 piece Kasseri cheese
   (or Parmesan cheese) for
   grating at the table

1 recipe Irresistible Mushrooms
   (page 99)

Add salt to a pot of 5 quarts of water and bring to a boil. While the water comes to a boil, chop the vegetables.

When the water boils, add the buckwheat noodles. Let the water return to a boil, and when the pasta is almost done (in about 8 minutes), add the chopped vegetables. When the pot returns to a boil and the vegetables are crisp-tender (in about 3 minutes), drain the pasta and vegetables thoroughly, shaking the colander to remove all the water. Return the food to the cooking pot to keep it hot, and drizzle with the oil and vinegar.

While the pasta is cooking, make the Irresistible Mushrooms. Toss them with the drained pasta and vegetables, and serve immediately. Pass the cheese at the table.

Yield: 4 to 6 servings

About Rice . . .

Rice is so primary to my family's diet, and to the diet of so many people, that I find it almost hard to discuss. Thinking about rice brings up feelings of gratitude and of sadness. If I could have one wish, it would be for rice in every person's bowl. In Chinese, the written character for "rice" is the same as the character for "food." Rice is that essential, that basic to the Chinese way of life. What one food could even suggest the vastness of our eating style in the West?

Rice is by nature brown. White rice has been refined; the bran and the germ have been removed, and along with it, much of the protein and most of the B vitamins and minerals. There are thousands of varieties of rice and they all are brown at harvest. While the enriching process does return some B vitamins to white rice, it is still deficient in fiber and still nutritionally inferior to the whole grain.

My rice of choice is short-grain brown, which is chewy and substantial. Since it is basic to my family's diet, I buy it organically grown. In this book, "rice" refers to organic short-grain brown rice, unless stated otherwise.

Basmati is another delicious variety of rice. Both brown and white basmati rice have particularly savory flavors and an indescribably appealing fragrance. An occasional bowl of white basmati with a succulent Indian curry makes a wonderful, light meal.

How to Cook Rice

Cooking rice is a simple process in which every detail is important. Attention to detail produces perfect rice — each grain separate, moist, and chewy.

For all types of rice, bring measured water to a boil in a pot with a tight-fitting lid while you rinse the rice in a bowl of water, discarding floating hulls, debris, and cloudy water. Drain cleaned rice in a strainer, and add it slowly to rapidly boiling water. This shocks the rice clear through, stimulating every molecule.

When the water and rice return to a rolling boil, let it boil for about a minute, then stir the pot, cover it, and reduce the heat to a simmer. For brown rice, cook 45 minutes; for white rice, cook 20 to 25 minutes.

Rice cooks best undisturbed, so don't lift the lid until time's up.

Proportions

To cook 1 cup rice use 1¾ to 2 cups water. (This is the trickiest amount of rice to cook. Be sure to use a sufficiently small pot, with a tight-fitting lid.)

To cook 2 cups rice use 3½ cups water.

To cook 3 to 30 cups rice use 1½ cups water per cup of rice.

To cook over 30 cups rice use several smaller pots.

. . . and the Other Whole Grains

Grains are the real fuel-food of human beings. They are rich in carbohydrates, which translates as energy. If a person were a car, carbohydrates would be gasoline. People all over the world depend on grains to keep them running.

Whole grains are the most vital of the grain foods. If you plant a whole grain, it will grow. But refined grains will not grow. They are missing their hull and their germ, two of the most vital parts. This is the case with white flour and white rice. They may be "enriched," but the full measure of what has been removed is never restored to the grain. Although they still offer some nutrition, it is not the full and potent package provided by nature.

In a brilliant leap forward, the most recent federal food recommendation chart puts whole grains at the base, or foundation, of the human diet pyramid. Not meat, but grains! This chapter explores the grains that comprise that base. In addition to rice, we have couscous, bulgar, barley, millet, buckwheat, corn, rye, oats, and others, available at many supermarkets and natural food stores. Each grain has its own unique personality; here are my favorites. The whole grains are marked with an asterisk.

Couscous

Couscous is the quickest to cook, and among the tastiest of grains. (It is a coarse grind of semolina wheat, the same grain from which pasta is made.) In France and Morocco, where couscous is extremely popular, a special cooker is used, and the grains are rubbed with butter and salt before being cooked. The following procedure is much easier and produces an equally delectable grain.

To make 3 servings, pour 1 cup boiling water over 1 cup of couscous, 1 tablespoon butter, and ½ teaspoon salt (or to taste). Cover tightly for 5 minutes, then use a fork to fluff up the small grains. If you don't fluff it up after 5 minutes, it will congeal irreparably into a solid mass.

Couscous is available in a whole wheat form, which is light brown in color, and a refined form, which is yellow. Whole wheat couscous has an earthy flavor; yellow couscous tastes similar to pasta.

Bulgur

Bulgur is another form of wheat; since it is cracked and partially cooked, it's quick to prepare, but it does take longer than couscous. Bulgur is most commonly known in the Middle Eastern dish, tabbouleh, where it is mixed with chopped parsley, tomatoes, and an olive oil vinaigrette.

To prepare 3 servings of bulgur, use a saucepan to bring 1½ cups water or bouillon with ½ teaspoon salt to a boil. Add 1 cup of bulgur, bring the water back to a boil, then cover the pot tightly and remove it from the heat. Let it stand 20 to 30 minutes, until all the water is absorbed, then fluff it with a fork.

Bulgur prepared this way is light in texture, yet more substantial to the bite than couscous. It has a coarse nuttiness, an appealing quality for grain salads and pilaf.

Barley

We know barley best in soup, where its hearty texture and slightly slippery quality provide substance and contrast to vegetables and beans. It takes a full hour to cook barley, whether in soup or with rice.

In cold weather, I cook barley and rice together. It's a chewy, warming combination that satisfies down to the bones. To make 6 servings, bring 3½ cups water (with 1 teaspoon salt, optional) to a boil, then add ½ cup barley. Let the water return to a simmer, then cover the pot and cook for 15 minutes. After 15 minutes, add 1½ cups of short grain brown rice. Let the water return to a simmer, cover the pot, and cook 40 to 45 minutes, covered. Don't open the pot until time's up.

I also like to use barley that has been ground to flour. It is light in color and taste, holds moisture well, and may be used in combination with rice flour to replace wheat flour in quick breads and muffins. (People who are allergic to wheat can still enjoy baked goods when this combination is used.)

*Millet

Of all the grains, millet is richest in nutrients and so tasty that the birds sing about it. But they eat it raw. Cooking "birdseed" to perfection can be tricky. Sometimes it ends up dry; sometimes mushy. I have adjusted both the water-grain ratio and the cooking time, but perfection continues to evade me. And I'm not alone — listen to the widely divergent opinions of other cookbook authors on the subject. From the shelf above my desk, one book recommends using 4 cups of water to cook one cup of millet, while another book says 1½ cups of water is plenty. The 4-cup author recommends 40 minutes of cooking; the one who uses 1½ cups of water cooks the millet only 15 to 20 minutes. Neither method worked for me.

One thing I know for sure: Millet tastes best when pan-roasted until fragrant before it is boiled. For 4 servings, pan-roast 1 cup of millet until fragrant (about 10 minutes) over medium-low heat. Place the roasted grain in a saucepan with a tight-fitting lid; add 2⅓ cups boiling water and ½ teaspoon salt. Bring to a boil over medium heat, then reduce the heat to a simmer and cover the pot. Simmer 25 to 30 minutes, until all the water has been absorbed. Keep your fingers crossed, and fluff the grain with a fork.

Because of its texture, I always serve millet with a very saucy stew on top, and it's always good. But not perfect . . . yet.

*Buckwheat

Whole buckwheat, known as kasha when it's roasted, is the strongest-flavored of the grains. Compared to the subtle flavors of the others, it doesn't even taste like a grain — and technically, it isn't. It's a grass. But you could fool my rice pot, and for all practical purposes, it's a grain in the same way that a tomato is a vegetable — because it behaves like one.

Like millet, cooked buckwheat tends toward mushiness. To prevent this, many chefs sauté the grain with an egg before adding the boiling water; I don't. I never found the technique effective, and I don't like egg in my grains.

To make 4 servings, sauté 1 cup buckwheat groats (roasted or not, as you like) in 2 tablespoons butter, stirring frequently, for 2 minutes. Add 2½ cups boiling water and ½ to 1 teaspoon salt; let the water return to a boil, cover the pot, and simmer for 30 minutes. Be sure the pot is really simmering; if the heat is too low, the grain will definitely be mushy.

The two things we enjoy most about buckwheat are buckwheat noodles (soba) and buckwheat pancakes. The strong flavor of the groat mellows delectably when it's ground to flour, and in that form, a person could happily eat buckwheat on a regular basis. We do; I buy soba noodles by the case.

Certain grains such as corn, rye, oats, and wheat berries rarely find their way to my table in their whole form. I find these grains more suitable when they're ground to meal or flour, or rolled. And no discussion of whole grains would be complete without mentioning popcorn, the rascal of the grain family. I love to eat it with soup.

Spicy Fried Rice

This is not a recipe to be forgotten; taste it once and you'll make it again and again. Spicy Fried Rice can be served with Thai, Mexican, Spanish, Greek, or Italian food and hold its own.

I was inspired to make this after tasting a particular version of Thai rice in which a strong, fermented sauce called patis *is used. It is truly a horrible-smelling liquid, based on fish, which somehow imparts an irresistible flavor to food. I've substituted a combination of soy sauce and ume plum vinegar here, and it works perfectly. But if you crave authenticity and aren't a strict vegetarian, give the fish sauce a try.*

Cook the rice for this dish in advance; it fries best when it's had a chance to cool.

3 tablespoons mild oil, such as canola
2 cups finely chopped onion
¾ teaspoon salt
1 tablespoon ume plum vinegar
1 tablespoon soy sauce
1 to 2 teaspoons Tabasco sauce
6 tablespoons tomato paste
scant ½ cup chopped scallions
¾ cup finely chopped Chinese parsley
4 cups cooked rice
1 ripe tomato, cut in wedges

Heat the oil in a wok or large frying pan. When it's hot, add the onion and cook until it's transparent.

Combine salt, vinegar, soy sauce, Tabasco, tomato paste, scallions and ½ cup of the Chinese parsley; set aside.

Add rice to wok; stir fry 3 minutes. Add tomato paste mixture and stir-fry 5 minutes on high heat.

Turn the rice onto a serving platter. Garnish with the remaining Chinese parsley and the tomato wedges. Serve immediately.

Yield: 4 to 5 servings

Walnut Rice Fontinella

Imagine a rice dish that tastes like a cross between pilaf and risotto, but is quicker to make; that's Walnut Rice Fontinella. It's quick because it's based on previously cooked rice, and it's elegant because it includes toasted walnuts and the Fontinella cheese. Fontinella is a semi-hard cheese, softer and creamier than Parmesan, but like Parmesan, easy to grate and long-lasting. It is slightly sharp and melts easily, so it combines well with grains like rice and pasta. It's good on pizza too. Festive fare doesn't come much easier than this.

½ cup walnuts

1½ tablespoons butter

4 cups previously cooked short-grain brown rice

1 tablespoon soy sauce

Scant ½ teaspoon salt

½ cup finely grated Fontinella cheese

3 tablespoons minced Italian parsley

Put the walnuts in a cold toaster oven and bake 10 minutes at 300 degrees. Chop them, but not too finely.

Melt the butter in a frying pan and when it's hot, add the rice. Use a spatula to keep the rice moving in the pan so it doesn't stick, and when it's almost hot, add the soy sauce and the salt. Mix well, then sprinkle in all the walnuts, most of the cheese and most of the parsley. Reserve a bit of each for a garnish.

Continue stirring until all is hot, then transfer to a warmed serving bowl. Garnish and serve immediately.

Yield: 4 servings

Green Rice

Green rice is striking in color, mild in taste, and goes with almost any menu.

On its own, it makes a lovely bed for steamed vegetables such as cauliflower, beets, yellow crook-neck squash, and carrots, whose colors stand out brightly against the parsley-green rice.

This dish is best made with rice that has cooled but has not been chilled. If time permits, cook the rice early in the day, and when it's done, tilt the cover so steam escapes from the pot; let it cool on the stovetop.

2 cups short-grain brown rice

3½ cups water

3 cups Italian parsley

3½ tablespoons oil (choose a mild oil or extra-virgin olive oil, depending on your menu)

⅓ cup finely grated Kasseri cheese (or freshly-grated Parmesan)

2 cloves garlic

1¾ teaspoons salt

2 teaspoons rice vinegar

To cook the rice, bring the water to a boil and add the grain. When the water begins to boil vigorously again, cover it, reduce the heat to a simmer, and cook 45 minutes without lifting the lid.

Blenderize the parsley, oil, cheese, garlic, salt, and vinegar to make a smooth, pesto-like purée. Use the "pulse" feature on the blender, and between pulses, move the parsley into the blender blades with a rubber spatula as necessary.

Heat a wok or large skillet. Pour in half the blended mixture and let it heat up; add the rice, and stir-fry it, breaking up clumps; add the remaining parsley mixture and continue stir-frying until everything is hot. Serve immediately, or put the rice in a casserole dish and keep it warm in a 250 degree oven until serving time.

Yield: 6 to 8 servings

Risotto

If you've eaten risotto, you probably know it as one of the most indulgent rice dishes of all time. It's often prepared with butter, cream, cheese, or all three. This recipe tastes as rich as risotto, yet uses only a tablespoon of cheese per serving.

4½ cups peeled and cubed pumpkin squash or butternut squash

2 cups uncooked brown rice

3½ cups water

2 teaspoons salt

½ cup minced parsley

½ cup grated Parmesan cheese

½ cup toasted pumpkin seeds or chopped, toasted walnuts

Place pumpkin, rice, water, and salt in a saucepan that allows at least 2 inches of headroom.

Bring to a boil, stir, cover, and reduce heat to a simmer. Cook 45 minutes over low heat without lifting the lid.

When rice is done, toss it into a large bowl containing the parsley, cheese, and nuts or seeds. Toss thoroughly and serve immediately.

Yield: 6 to 8 servings

Thai Yellow Rice

Only recently did I have the pleasure of tasting authentic Thai Yellow Rice, and it was so good I ended up pushing the two vegetable dishes to the side so I could enjoy it on its own. The challenge with this dish is pairing it successfully with other foods. Usually rice is the background, a bland receptacle for tasty sauces. Here, where it holds its own, other dishes must be selected to complement rather than overpower it.

2 cups uncooked white basmati rice, rinsed well

I teaspoon salt

3½ cups boiling water

1½ cups (12 ounces) coconut milk (canned or frozen, thawed)

2 curry leaves, lime leaves, or bay leaves

¼ teaspoon ginger powder

I teaspoon turmeric

½ to I teaspoon salt (I use the full measure)

Cook the rice in the boiling water with salt for 20 minutes. Remove the cooked rice from the pot and in it, heat the coconut milk with the leaves, ginger, turmeric, and salt. When the coconut milk begins to boil, add the cooked rice and let the coconut milk return to a boil. Cook uncovered for an additional 15 minutes, using a "flame tamer" (asbestos pad) under the pot to diffuse the heat.

Yield: 4 to 6 servings

Garlic-Hijiki Rice

This simple dish is as satisfying as it is basic. It's perfect after the holidays, when a return to ordinary fare feels extraordinarily good. Make it with fresh or previously cooked rice.

3½ cups water
2 cups brown rice
I teaspoon salt
4 cups boiling water
I cup dried hijiki
I tablespoon mild oil, such as canola
3 cloves pressed garlic
I½ tablespoons soy sauce (or more to taste)
Toasted sesame seeds

Bring the 3½ cups water to a rolling boil, then add the rice and salt. When the water returns to a boil, stir it gently, cover, and reduce heat to a simmer. Cook for 45 minutes, undisturbed.

Once the rice is cooking, pour 4 cups boiling water over the hijiki; just let it soak until the rice is finished.

When the rice is done, heat the oil in a wok or very large skillet. Add the garlic and sauté it for a minute or two, until it's golden, then add the rice. Lift the hijiki from its soaking water (this leaves any sand behind) into a strainer, and shake out the excess water. Chop the strands of hijiki if they're too long to eat easily; add to the wok. Stir-fry the mixture until it's hot, adding soy sauce in the process. When everything's hot, the dish is done. Garnish with toasted sesame seeds.

Yield: 6 servings

There's one more unusual inhabitant in our kitchen – the refrigerator. It's a petite, Swiss-made model which provides a paltry 8 cubic feet of refrigeration space. It is, in fact, ridiculously small, but it's claim to fame is great: silence. It doesn't defrost itself, it makes no drinking water, no ice – and absolutely no noise.

Semolina Fresca

This is the quickest-cooking pilaf on record, and a deliciously light alternative to rice. It's as beautiful to the eye as it is to the palate and as colorful as it is delicious.

1½ tablespoons extra-virgin olive oil
⅔ cup coarsely grated carrot
⅔ cup coarsely grated zucchini
I tablespoon red wine vinegar
1½ tablespoons butter
2 cups boiling water
I teaspoon salt
2 cups couscous
I ripe tomato, finely chopped
¼ cup minced Italian parsley
⅓ cup pitted and finely chopped Kalamata olives (optional)
2 tablespoons extra-virgin olive oil
I tablespoon ume plum vinegar

Heat the olive oil in a large, heavy skillet, and when it's hot, sauté the carrot and zucchini for 1 minute. While over the heat, add the vinegar, butter, boiling water, and salt. When the butter has melted, turn off the heat. Mix well and add the couscous. Press the couscous down into the liquid and cover the pan tightly for 5 minutes.

Fluff the couscous with a large fork, and toss in the tomato, parsley, and olives, reserving a bit of each to garnish the top. Drizzle with the remaining olive oil and the ume plum vinegar; toss lightly. Garnish and serve hot.

Yield: 6 servings

. . . .

SUGGESTED MENU
Green Salad with Honey-Mustard Vinaigrette
Grilled Tofu
Semolina Fresca
Oregon Beets

. . . .

Baked Bulgur Pilaf

If I were in charge of the English language, I'd change the name of this nutty, flavorful grain. "Bulgur" sounds so heavy and dense. Fortunately, there's "Pilaf" after it. To my ear, pilaf is what this dish is about — lightness, with a touch of the exotic.

The casserole takes less than ten minutes to assemble, then it bakes for 30 minutes at low heat.

2 tablespoons butter

1 clove pressed or minced garlic

½ pound mushrooms, washed, dried, and sliced

1½ teaspoons salt (or to taste)

2 cups bulgur

1 8-ounce can sliced water chestnuts

3 cups boiling water

½ cup finely minced parsley (preferably Italian)

Preheat the oven to 250 degrees. Melt the butter in a skillet, and sauté the garlic and mushrooms 4 to 5 minutes, adding salt at the end.

In a 2-quart baking dish with a tight-fitting lid, combine the sautéed mixture, the bulgur, the water chestnuts, and the boiling water. Stir well, cover quickly, and place in the preheated oven.

Bake 30 minutes, until all the water is absorbed. Toss in the minced parsley and serve.

Yield: 6 servings

Vegetables

The beauty of vegetables has to do with their intricacy, their variety, and with their mystery. For all our technological savvy, who can invent a vegetable? (Don't mention "broccoflower" as an example. It's an abomination, as any lover of vegetables would agree.)

The produce section should be the most interesting section of the market; if that's not your experience, you may be shopping at the wrong store. Take a good look. Are there organic fruits and vegetables to select? Are you seeing the best produce your area has to offer?

Where produce is concerned, shop first for freshness. Truly fresh vegetables and fruits have a special quality that is apparent at first glance; they stand out from the rest. Size is also important. Certain vegetables, like green beans, cucumbers, and zucchini, are unquestionably more appealing when they're small. I'm not talking about "baby" vegetables, which are overpriced and too cutesy for my taste, but fullgrown specimens that were harvested young. They're more tender and less watery than their larger siblings, and they're charming served whole on the plate. Other great items like kabocha pumpkins, butternut squash, and watermelons, for example, can be big and beautiful, inside and out. The large ones offer greater value on a per pound basis because there is less waste from peel and seed.

Whatever you're attracted to, be sure to really look at your choices. Until I've inspected my dinner-to-be from every angle, I'm not satisfied. When I'm lax at the store, I end up noticing the bruised apples and infested broccoli once they're home.

Vegetables don't need elaborate treatment to make them palatable. When they're grown organically and harvested at their prime, the clean flavor is best enhanced by simple cooking techniques such as steaming, wok-cooking, grilling, and roasting. Experimenting in the kitchen quickly teaches that eggplants respond better to the grill than to the steamer, and that over-boiling cabbage "makes stink," as we say in Hawaii. But even in the process of learning, it's hard to ruin a good vegetable unless you overcook it entirely.

A simply cooked vegetable is usually delicous with just a dab of butter, with small splashes of olive oil and ume plum vinegar or lemon juice, or with a complementary sauce. Trying new sauces over steamed vegetables is a wonderful way to taste them both.

And one last thought about less common vegetables like banana squash, burdock root, and parsnips, and about less common varieties — like Yellow Finn potatoes, golden beets, and Italian parsley: These are vegetables I brought home from the store without having tried before. I'm glad I did.

Don't Cry or How to Chop an Onion

It is possible to chop or dice an onion without shedding a tear. This method does not involve a match in the mouth but it involves knowing why onions make you cry in the first place.

We cry when essential onion oil escapes into the air in the form of vapors. This happens when onions are cut. The more cut surface exposed, the more vapors waft eyewards. Obviously, the trick is to avoid this.

Some small amount of vapor is released in the peeling of the onion, so super-sensitive individuals may want to do that part under water (just the onion, thanks). Cut off both ends and peel away the skin.

From here on, the trick is to keep the onion together without exposing cut surfaces. It's easy with practice; the degree of ease depends upon the particular onion and on how finely it needs to be chopped. Naturally, a coarse chop requires the least effort.

Cut the peeled onion in half lengthwise and quickly lay the two halves on the cut edge. First, slice in one direction, holding the onion with your free hand so it doesn't separate. Turn the onion and cut across the first slices, still holding it together gently.

Space cuts widely for a coarse chop, closely for a fine dice.

Properly done, you still have the shape of two onion halves before you. Leave them like that, cut but intact, until they're used. Once they hit the pan, heat transforms the vapors, and instead of tears you'll have the incomparable smell of onions cooking.

The Simple Art of Stir-Fry or May Your Wok Be Always Hot

We enjoy wok-cooking so much that we installed a separate burner on the stovetop for our bowl-shaped skillet. It's always set up, ready to use. There are also two big woks hanging on the wall, in case company comes. One feeds forty; the other, seventy-five. The big ones are really for catering, but we like the look of them, so we keep them at home when they're off duty. The smallest wok lives on the spice shelf. It's three inches in diameter, and came to me one Christmas in a box with air holes labeled "Pet Wok."

The wok is like a combination skillet and saucepan, but it holds more than either one. Its sloping sides make stir-frying easy, and spilling practically impossible. In it, you can cook a maximum of food in a minimum of oil.

Stir-fry technique is simple. First, you heat the wok. This is essential. A cold wok is sleeping; it must be wakened by heat. Then add a bit of oil — the Chinese pour the oil in a circle about mid-way between the edge and the bottom of the hot wok. As the oil runs to the bottom, it greases the bowl of the vessel. Once hot and oiled, it's ready to cook.

All the vegetables must be chopped in advance. Add them in gradual sequence, with the longest-cooking variety (like cauliflower) going in first. Keep the heat high and stir almost constantly. Add the other vegetables according to the time they'll take to cook to (your version of) perfection. This will also depend on the size of the pieces. Last in line are quick-cookers like sweet red pepper slivers, green onions, and any other vegetables cut in a fine julienne.

Wok-cooking may or may not reflect an Oriental influence. Here are a few ideas to illustrate how varied stir-fries may be.

- Stir-fry celery, zucchini, bamboo shoots, Chinese peas, water chestnuts, and bean sprouts. At the last minute, add Chinese Brown Sauce (page 66). Serve this over brown rice, with Grilled Tofu (page 116).

- Stir-fry onion, eggplant, red and green peppers, basil, and shiitake mushrooms. Serve over finely slivered green cabbage with rice, fried tempeh, and Peanut Sauce (page 62) over all.

- Stir-fry onions, potatoes (previously baked potatoes are perfect), carrots, mushrooms, and broccoli. Serve alongside Spinach Nutloaf with Béchamel Nouvelle (pages 114 and 63) and a fresh green salad.

Chinese Vegetables in the Wok

Don't be put off by how ordinary this recipe sounds. It's a particularly good combination of vegetables, and the simple sauce is a classic.

For a satisfying and slightly exotic meal, serve Chinese Vegetables with rice, Oriental Noodle Salad, and Tofu Patties (pages 38 and 118).

For the Vegetables:

1 tablespoon mild oil (peanut oil is traditional but any mild oil is fine)

1 tablespoon fresh hot pepper, such as a jalapeño, seeded and thinly sliced

1 tablespoon Chinese black beans (see page 190)

½ pound green beans (about 2 cups)

1 medium carrot (to make ⅔ cup julienne)

½ pound won bok (Chinese cabbage) (about 2 cups)

3 scallions

For the Sauce:

2 tablespoons soy sauce

2 tablespoons rice vinegar

1 tablespoon honey

½ teaspoon salt

1 tablespoon toasted sesame oil

Combine sauce ingredients and set aside. Now, on to the dreaded peppers. Be sure to protect your fingers by wearing rubber gloves or by avoiding the hot parts. Once sliced, place the pepper on a small plate. Rinse and mince the black beans; place them on the plate with the peppers.

Wash, trim, and cut the green beans in 1-inch diagonal pieces. Bring a small pot of water to a boil, and boil the beans 3 minutes; drain; keep uncovered. Cut the won bok in ½-inch pieces across the leaves.

Cut the carrot in a fine julienne, and cut the scallions lengthwise, then in 1-inch diagonal pieces. Now that everything is assembled, heat the wok on high; add the oil and get it hot.

Stir-fry the pepper and black beans for 1 minute on high, then add the carrot; stir-fry another minute, then add the beans and won bok. Stir-fry until the won bok is limp (2 to 3 minutes), then add the sauce and scallions. Stir-fry 1 more minute and serve immediately.

Yield: 4 to 6 servings

Stir-fry Zucchini with Cashews

There are only two things to know about zucchini — choose small, fresh ones, and don't overcook them. The beauty of this popular summer squash is its tender, juicy-yet-firm flesh. My zucchini of choice is no longer than five inches, and just an inch in diameter. The skin is shiny and uniformly patterned. At this, the adolescent vegetable's prime, the seeds are small, the skin thin, and the flavor sharp.

This simple Oriental side dish is good in the summer, when small zucchinis are abundant. Don't try it with any zukes over 6 inches long or more than 1½ inches in diameter; the recipe's success depends on fresh and tender vegetables.

⅔ cup raw cashew nuts

6 young zucchini, cut in ⅓-inch rounds

1 tablespoon mild oil, such as canola

2 teaspoons fresh ginger, peeled and finely grated

1 teaspoon sesame seeds

Salt

3 scallions, cut in 1-inch diagonal pieces

½ cup finely slivered sweet red pepper

½ cup finely slivered yellow bell pepper

Roast the cashews 10 minutes, or until fragrant, at 300 degrees. I use the toaster oven without preheating it. While the nuts roast, cut the zucchini, scallions, and peppers and grate the ginger.

In a wok or 10-inch skillet, heat the oil until it is very hot. Toss the zucchini in the hot oil until each piece is coated, then add the ginger and sesame seeds. Keep the heat high. Toss well and sprinkle everything with salt to taste. Stir-fry 2 minutes. Add the scallions and peppers, and continue cooking, stirring constantly until everything is done. Toss in the cashews and serve immediately.

Yield: 4 to 6 servings

Stir-fry Broccoli with Mushrooms

Simple stir-fries like this, with just a couple of favorite vegetables, are quick to make and are always well received.

1 large head broccoli (3 to 4 cups chopped)
½ pound small mushrooms
1½ teaspoons mild oil, such as canola
2 tablespoons butter
2 cloves garlic, minced or pressed
1 tablespoon water
1 teaspoon kuzu or cornstarch (approximately)
2 tablespoons soy sauce

Wash the broccoli and cut off the tough portion of the base. Peel the remaining stem and chop it finely; cut the broccoli flower into small bite-sized florets. Wash the mushrooms, drain them thoroughly, and cut them in half.

Heat the oil and 1 tablespoon of the butter in a large skillet or wok. Add the broccoli and garlic and stir-fry 3 to 5 minutes over medium heat until the vegetable is half-tender.

Separately, dissolve the kuzu or cornstarch in the water, and keep it handy. This thickener measurement is approximate here because it depends on the amount of liquid the mushrooms release. If more thickener is needed, just dissolve it in the smallest possible amount of water, and add it to the pan.

Add the remaining butter and the mushrooms to the skillet. Increase the heat, and stir-fry 3 minutes or until the mushrooms are almost cooked. Sprinkle the soy sauce over all and keep stir-frying. The mushrooms will release their juices, creating liquid in the pan. Add the thickener-water mixture and stir until the liquid thickens. Serve immediately.

Yield: 3 to 4 servings

Stir-fry Hijiki *and* Vegetables

This simple stir-fry includes — but is not dominated by — hijiki, a noodle-like, cal-cium-rich vegetable of the sea. If you're not yet a hijiki fan, this recipe is a good place to begin. You'll discover its full, yet mild flavor, and how easily it mingles with vege-tables of the land. Serve this atop brown rice with Grilled Tofu (page 116) and steamed butternut squash.

For the Sauce:

6 tablespoons soy sauce

1½ teaspoons honey

2 tablespoons sherry or mirin (sweet rice wine)

2½ tablespoons rice vinegar

2 teaspoons toasted sesame oil

¼ teaspoon salt (optional)

1 tablespoon plus 2 teaspoons kuzu (or 1 tablespoon plus 1 teaspoon cornstarch)

For the Rest:

3 tablespoons whole (not hulled) sesame seeds

½ ounce hijiki (about ¾ cup dry)

4 cups boiling water

1 medium onion

2 cloves garlic

1 tablespoon peeled and finely grated ginger root

2 medium carrots (to make 1 cup roll-cut carrots)

½ a cauliflower (2 cups chopped)

1 large or 2 medium heads broccoli (4 cups bite-sized florets, and about 2 cups finely chopped stems)

1 sweet red pepper

1½ tablespoons mild oil, such as canola

Combine sauce ingredients; stir well and set aside.

Toast the sesame seeds 10 minutes at 300 degrees; reserve.

Pour boiling water generously over the hijiki; reserve that too. Cut the onion into thin half-moons; slice or press the garlic; peel and grate the ginger; roll-cut the carrots; chop the cauliflower into bite-sized pieces; chop the broccoli, also bite-size; and sliver the pepper.

Heat the oil in a wok or large skillet and in it, sauté the onion, garlic, and ginger for 3 to 5 minutes over medium-high heat. Add the carrots and cauliflower and mix well. Cover the pan for 5 minutes, stirring twice, then add the broccoli stems and stir-fry 2 minutes. Add the broccoli florets and red pepper. Lift the hijiki from its soaking water and add it to the wok.

Scoop ½ cup from the top of the hijiki soaking water and add it to the sauce mixture. Stir-fry the hijiki and vegetables, covering and uncovering, for about 4 minutes (until everything is nearly done), then stir the sauce, and add it.

Cook until the sauce has thickened and the vegetables are done to perfection. Serve immediately with rice, topped with a sprinkling of sesame seeds. Pass remaining seeds at the table.

Yield: 4 to 6 servings

Kale with Garlic and Parmesan

It would take a whole bunch of store-bought kale to yield one generous serving of this dish. I make it when our garden kale is at its peak and there is more than I can use. For the sake of this recipe, I'm assuming that you, too, have access to a carload of kale. Because if you ever do, you'll want to taste it this way.

Another idea: halve the recipe and serve small portions.

12 cups kale (mid-rib removed), washed and coarsley chopped, packed tightly into measuring cup
6 cloves garlic
1 tablespoon olive oil
1 tablespoon extra-virgin olive oil
¼ teaspoon salt
¼ cup freshly grated Parmesan cheese

Steam the kale in a huge pot over boiling water until tender, about 30 minutes.

Slice the garlic cloves, and just before the kale is done, heat the olive oil in a wok or skillet and fry the garlic until it browns. Remove it from the pan (discard it), reserving the oil. Remove the kale from the large pot and put it in the hot oil. Toss it thoroughly, sprinkle it with the salt, add the extra-virgin olive oil, cover, and cook 5 more minutes, tossing several times. Toss in the cheese, cover, and cook 3 minutes more. Put it in a serving bowl and bring it to the table.

It's already reduced itself considerably. Now watch it disappear.

Yield: 3 to 4 servings

Irresistible Mushrooms

I use Irresistible Mushrooms as a topping for many dishes: mashed potatoes, Italian Tofu Steaks (page 121), and Spinach Nutburgers (page 114), to name a few. The beauty of this recipe is its simplicity, and the realization, upon tasting it, that mushrooms don't need butter to be delicious. I call the technique used to achieve this feat water-sauté, and I use it often to reduce or eliminate fat.

You'll notice that there are only four ingredients in the recipe (and one of them is water). Such simplicity results in a topping that celebrates the quintessential mushroom flavor.

¼ cup water
½ pound mushrooms, sliced ¼-inch thick
2 tablespoons soy sauce
1 teaspoon kuzu (or ⅔ teaspoon cornstarch) dissolved in 2 teaspoons water

Heat the ¼ cup water in a skillet, and when it boils, add the mushrooms. Sauté the mushrooms in water for about 3 minutes, until they begin to soften and turn a shade darker in color. While they cook, dissolve the kuzu (or cornstarch) in the 2 teaspoons water.

Add soy sauce to the pan, and sauté the mushrooms for about 2 minutes more, or until they are almost done to your taste. Add the thickener dissolved in water; stir until the liquid thickens. Remove the pan from the heat, and serve immediately.

Yield: 2 to 4 servings

Oregon Beets

There are only 3 main ingredients in this recipe: beets, hazelnuts, and fresh rosemary. When the nuts are roasted, their brown skins slip off easily; the creamy white interior provides a striking contrast to the crimson beets and piney-green rosemary. Despite its simplicity, this is a festive dish to present.

10 small beets (about 1½ pounds)
7 sprigs fresh rosemary, 2 to 3 inches long each
2 tablespoons lemon juice
⅓ cup whole hazelnuts
2 tablespoons extra-virgin olive oil
1 tablespoon balsamic vinegar
2 tablespoons fresh orange juice
⅓ teaspoon salt

Boil the beets whole, with peel, in water to cover, with 2 sprigs of rosemary and the lemon juice. Once the water has boiled, reduce the heat to a simmer and cover the pot. Depending on the size of the beets, they will be tender in 25 to 45 minutes. Test them after 25 minutes by probing one with a sharp knife. When the knife goes in easily, it's done.

Bake the hazelnuts 10 minutes at 300 degrees in an unpreheated toaster oven; cool them, then remove the skins by rubbing the nuts between two towels. Chop the nuts in half and reserve.

In a frying pan, combine the olive oil, vinegar, orange juice, and salt.

When the beets are done, plunge them in cool water and slip the skins off. Slice the beets in ¼- to ⅛-inch thick pieces.

Heat the olive oil mixture in the frying pan, and when it's hot, add the beets. Simmer for 2 minutes, then pour them into a warmed serving dish. Garnish with the 5 sprigs of rosemary and the chopped nuts. Serve immediately.

Yield: 4 to 6 servings

Memorable Mashed Potatoes

My mother makes extraordinary mashed potatoes, and her technique is simple: plenty of butter and sour cream. In this recipe, which still surprises me with its resemblance to hers, I've substituted creamy, blenderized tofu for the sour cream, and cut way back on the butter. The tofu taste is mild beyond recognition, but its creamy quality remains. Try it.

3 pounds russet potatoes
1 package firm, silken tofu
¼ cup butter
2 teaspoons salt
Pepper grinder for the table

Peel the potatoes, cut them in quarters, and put them in a pot of cold water. Bring the water to a boil, then reduce the heat and simmer until the potatoes are tender, about 15 minutes. The potatoes are tender when a fork goes in easily.

Drain the potatoes, reserving 2 tablespoons cooking water. Chop the butter and toss it with the hot potatoes; keep them covered.

Blenderize the tofu and the reserved potato cooking water until creamy. You'll need to stop a time or two and move the mixture around with a rubber spatula. Meanwhile, mash the potatoes in the pot. When they are lump-free, add the creamy tofu and the salt. Mix well, and they're ready to serve. Pass the pepper grinder at the table.

Yield: 6 to 8 servings

Creamy Mexican Potatoes

Creamy, spicy, and simple to make, this dish is based on small, freshly baked potatoes. They're cut in half lengthwise and topped with a creamy tofu sauce (it tastes like sour cream), then a second topping of salsa. For a simple meal, serve Creamy Mexican Potatoes with a fresh green salad and an ear of garden corn.

2½ pounds small potatoes, any type
1 package firm, silken tofu
2 tablespoons extra-virgin olive oil
1 tablespoon soy sauce
1½ teaspoons red wine vinegar
1 teaspoon olive oil
Salt and pepper
¾ to 1 cup fresh salsa, purchased or homemade (don't use the kind from a bottle here)
⅓ cup Chinese parsley (optional)

Scrub the potatoes, poke them with the point of a sharp knife so they don't explode, and bake them until done (about 45 minutes at 350 degrees).

While the potatoes bake, blenderize the tofu, the extra-virgin olive oil, soy sauce, and red wine vinegar. The mixture is thick, so stop the blender a couple of times and use the rubber spatula to guide the mixture into the blades.

Use the 1 teaspoon of olive oil to grease an 8-inch by 12-inch baking pan. When the potatoes are baked, remove them from the oven and cut them in half lengthwise. Place them in the oiled pan, salt them generously, and pepper them sparingly. Spread the tofu sauce over them evenly; spread the salsa atop the tofu sauce, and bake the potatoes another 15 minutes, until the toppings are hot. Sprinkle with the Chinese parsley, if desired, and serve.

Yield: 6 servings

Pressure-Steamed Vegetables
with Olive Oil and Ume Plum Vinegar

The pressure cooker softens and mellows vegetables more than simple steaming or sautéing — in about a quarter of the time. I find vegetables prepared this way ultimately comforting because all the textures are smooth, with no rough edges.

Any variety of coarse vegetables may be used here, and the more the better. If rutabagas or turnips were available in my area, I'd try them too. Be sure to cut the vegetables in equal chunks so they'll all be done at the same time.

I bunch kale (about 10 large leaves)

2 large onions

2 large carrots

2 medium sweet potatoes or 2 large russets

2 medium beets

Half a medium cabbage

2 medium avocados

Extra-virgin olive oil and ume plum vinegar to taste (no substitutions please)

Fresh black pepper

Place a steamer basket in the pressure cooker. Add water beneath (not touching) the basket. Remove stalks from the kale and chop the leaves coarsely. Put the kale in the pressure cooker. Peel the onions and quarter them. Scrub the carrots and chop coarsley. Peel the potatoes and beets and cut them in chunks, and cut the cabbage in thick wedges. Place these vegetables atop the kale.

Prepare the pressure cooker to cook, and turn the heat to high. Cook 7 minutes at medium pressure. When time's up, reduce pressure in the cooker immediately according to the cooker's instruction booklet and transfer the vegetables to a serving platter. Cut the avocadoes open and spoon the flesh atop; drizzle generously with olive oil, and sparingly with ume plum vinegar. Grind pepper over all; serve immediately.

Yield: 4 to 6 servings

Savory Vegetables

In this simple recipe vegetables are cooked in the oven in a tightly-lidded dish or casserole. The word "casserole" is rarely understood in its original sense any more, that is, as a cooking method in which foods are basted in their own juices along with small amounts of flavorful liquids.

Casseroling is a fabulous way to tenderize foods of dense texture such as potatoes, sweet potatoes, carrots, beets, burdock root and parsnips. It also brings out the best in onions and whole cloves of garlic.

Savory Vegetables are just that: vegetables cooked to perfection. They're not fancy, but they sure taste good.

1¾ pounds mixed vegetables, selected from the list above

2 tablespoons extra-virgin olive oil

2 tablespoons soy sauce

1 tablespoon balsamic vinegar

1 tablespoon mirin (Japanese rice sweetener) or sherry

2 to 4 sprigs fresh rosemary or sage (optional)

Preheat oven to 350 degrees. Prepare vegetables by peeling them and cutting into larger-than-bite-sized chunks. A roll-cut works well, keeps the shapes interesting, and makes the final presentation attractive.

Combine cut vegetables with the oil, soy sauce, vinegar, and mirin in your casserole dish, mixing well so the vegetables are all coated with liquid. Add 2 sprigs of herbs (if desired), cover, and place in the oven. Bake 1 to 1½ hours, basting 3 times. (Precise baking time depends on the size of your vegetable chunks.) Remove cooked herbs and garnish with the fresh ones just before serving.

Yield: 5 servings

So it is, when the new moon sets, and later, when the trillion stars arise, the crickets, the geck- os, and the drone of Hawaiian bullfrogs are the only sounds we hear. And we remember what drew us to Maui in the first place . . .

Basic Curried Vegetables

This is an easy curry, relatively low in fat, and one which calls for 5 vegetables: onions, potatoes, peas, and two of your choice. It's enjoyable to mix the spices for this dish; each adds its particular fragrance and flavor, and when they're combined, you've made your own curry powder.

1 medium onion

2 large potatoes (to make about 3½ cups chopped)

1 teaspoon turmeric

1 teaspoon ground cumin seed

2 teaspoons ground coriander seed

½ teaspoon dry mustard

¼ teaspoon ginger powder

Dash of cinnamon

1½ tablespoons mild oil, such as canola

1½ tablespoons butter

1½ cups water

2 cups vegetable of choice (eggplant, for example)

2 cups vegetable of choice (green beans, for example)

½ cup water

1 tablespoon whole wheat flour or garbanzo bean flour

½ cup yogurt

10 ounces frozen peas, thawed

1 teaspoon salt (or more to taste)

¼ teaspoon cayenne pepper (or more to taste)

Chop the onion and potatoes. Combine the turmeric, cumin, coriander, mustard, ginger, and cinnamon in a small bowl. Heat the oil and butter in a very large skillet or shallow pot, and add the mixed spices, frying until they bubble. Add the onion and potatoes, mix well, and add the 1½ cups water. When the water boils, reduce the heat, cover the pot, and simmer, covered, for 10 minutes. Chop the remaining vegetables.

Mix in the vegetables of choice, cover, and cook 15 minutes more.

Blenderize or whisk together the ½ cup water, the flour, and the yogurt. Add it to the vegetable pot and mix well. When it's hot, add the thawed peas. When they have heated through, and all the other vegetables are tender, season the curry to taste with salt and cayenne. Serve it hot over rice.

Yield: 6 to 8 servings

Spinach Balls with Tahini-Garlic Sauce

These spicy two-bite Spinach Balls are much lighter than their falafel cousins, but they're not opposed to being served the same way — in a warm pita pocket lined with lettuce and tomato. They make a great lunch or a hearty snack.

For the Spinach Balls:

- 1 10-ounce package frozen chopped spinach, thawed
- 1 pound firm tofu
- ½ cup garbanzo bean flour (sold in natural food stores)
- ½ cup minced onion
- ⅓ cup minced celery
- 1 tablespoon fine, fresh curry powder
- 1 tablespoon soy sauce
- 2 teaspoons seasoned salt

For the Tahini-Garlic Sauce:

- ⅓ cup raw tahini (sesame butter)
- ⅓ cup water
- 1 clove pressed garlic
- ½ teaspoon salt
- 2 teaspoons lemon juice

Squeeze the water from the spinach until it is almost but not totally dry, then place it in a mixing bowl, pulling it apart lightly. Towel-dry the tofu, then put it in the bowl with the spinach. Add the garbanzo flour, onion, celery, curry powder, soy sauce, and salt. Mash everything together with your fingers to an even consistency.

Preheat oven to 350 degrees.

Oil a cookie sheet lightly. Use a ¼-cup measure to scoop out cupfuls of the spinach mixture. Divide each scoop in two, and form two walnut-sized balls. Place them on the cookie sheet and bake for 40 minutes.

While the Spinach Balls bake, place all the sauce ingredients in a small bowl and mix thoroughly. Serve the hot Spinach Balls drizzled with Tahini Garlic Sauce.

Yield: 4 to 6 servings (24 Spinach Balls)

Spinach Curry

Rich, golden, and as hot or mild as you like, Spinach Curry is a tasty and satisfying dish. If you prefer a less rich curry, it's easy to substitute a mixture of yogurt, water, and whole wheat flour for the coconut milk, using the proportions below.

3½ cups (slightly more than
    I pound) peeled, diced potato

½ teaspoon salt

½ cup water

I tablespoon mild oil, such as
    canola

I tablespoon butter

4 to 6 cloves pressed or minced
    garlic

2½ teaspoons finely grated, peeled
    fresh ginger

I small onion, chopped

I teaspoon ground cumin seed

I teaspoon ground coriander seed

3 to 5 teaspoons curry powder, the
    freshest and finest available

3½ cups (about ¾ pound) diced
    eggplant, preferably the long,
    thin, Japanese type, cut in
    ½-inch pieces

½ cup water

I 10-ounce package frozen
    spinach, thawed and squeezed
    dry (or 2 pounds fresh spinach,
    well washed, dried, and chopped

1½ cups coconut milk (or 1¼ cup
    yogurt plus ¼ cup water and
    2 teaspoons whole wheat flour)

Salt to taste

Cayenne pepper to taste

To begin, prep the vegetables, including the garlic and ginger. Then simmer the potato, salt, and ½ cup water 15 minutes, covered, or until the potato is soft and the water has evaporated.

Separately, in a large skillet, heat the oil and butter. Sauté the garlic, ginger, onion, cumin, coriander, and curry powder for 1 minute; add the eggplant and toss well, coating it lightly with the spice mixture. Add the cooked potatoes and the second ½ cup of water; cover and cook on low 15 minutes, or until the eggplant is tender.

Add the spinach and the coconut milk or yogurt mixture. (If you are using fresh spinach, cover the pan and let it cook down. If it is frozen spinach, just heat it through.) Stir everything well. Season the curry to taste with additional salt, curry powder, and/or cayenne pepper.

Yield: 6 to 8 servings

Candied Yam or Sweet Potato Casserole

I've always loved candied yams but was never able to make them as well as my mother. I thought it couldn't be done without brown sugar. But it can . . . the secret to making perfect candied yams is to start with cooked potatoes. (It took years for me to figure that out.)

Actually, I prefer sweet potatoes to yams in this recipe; they're denser and hold their shape better. Bake them in their jackets the day before you want to make the casserole, and chill them overnight. Putting the casserole together the next day takes only 15 to 20 minutes.

6 cups baked, sliced yams or sweet potatoes (peeled)

¼ cup to ½ cup maple syrup (depending on your sweet tooth)

¼ cup honey

3 tablespoons butter

1 teaspoon salt

2 tablespoons cornstarch or 3 tablespoons kuzu

1 cup water

Use 1 tablespoon of the butter to grease a 7-inch by 11-inch baking dish. Lay the sliced potatoes slightly overlapping in the dish.

On the stovetop, combine the maple syrup, the honey, the remaining 2 tablespoons butter, the salt, and ½ cup water in a saucepan over medium heat. Dissolve the cornstarch or kuzu in the remaining ½ cup water, and when the pan mixture begins to boil gently, add the thickener. Stir until the sauce thickens, and remove from heat.

Pour the sauce over the sweet potatoes and bake until bubbly (20 to 25 minutes) at 350 degrees.

There's really nothing else to say about this dish, except you'll probably wish you'd made more. Everyone loves it.

Yield: 6 servings

Entrées

What is there to eat?'' is probably the most frequently asked question of the freshman vegetarian year. Those of us who've been raised on meat, fish, and chicken rightly wonder what's left when you erase those three items from the menu.

I'm happy to say that there's a lot left — more possibilities, in fact, than most carnivores imagine or ever experience. Like my own house in the country, the vegetarian castle is larger on the inside than it looks from the outside. And you never know what's in there until you open the door . . . but before we entrée, I want to say a few words about protein.

As you know, protein is the substance needed by the human body to build and maintain its tissues. Protein is not what we use for fuel (that's the function of carbohydrates); it's what we use for growth, maintenance, and repair. Protein is essential, to be sure, but not necessarily central to the diet.

In the Western tradition, a meal's main dish is taken to mean the "protein" dish. Sometimes this is not the case with vegetarian meals. Sometimes protein foods are sprinkled throughout a vegetarian meal, and there's not an identifiable "main" dish at all. Imagine this dinner, for example: vegetable salad with marinated beans and sunflower seeds, baked potato with broccoli and melted cheese, and nut-crusted pumpkin pie. Beans, seeds, cheese, and nuts — plenty of protein — but no clear-cut main dish. While not the typical vegetarian dinner, this is an interesting possibility and a format worth considering.

The more predictable meatless meal focuses on one of the protein sources below.

Vegetarians eat beans of all kinds and colors. Because they're abundant, inexpensive, and delicious, beans are as basic to the flesh-free diet as they are to ethnic cuisines around the world. Their variety is astounding. Beans can be marinated, stewed, mashed, refried, blended smooth into dips and pâtés, fermented, even made into entirely new products like tempeh and tofu.

What else do vegetarians eat? Casseroles like lasagna, enchilada, and pastitsio; nut loaves; all manner of curries; stuffed vegetables; stir-fries; and much, much more. These savory dishes may or may not contain eggs or cheese. Vegetarians who eat neither eggs nor dairy products (vegans) may want to substitute egg-replacer, soy margarine and/or soy cheese in some of the following recipes; everywhere I've tried to do so, it has worked out fine (with minor textural changes).

Another prime source of vegetarian protein is nuts and seeds. Before I explored vegetarian cuisine, the only times I ate nuts were on holidays and on airplanes. But nuts and seeds are among the most potent small packages the plant kingdom provides — especially when they're fresh. One benefit of shopping in a full-service natural food store is that the nuts and seeds do tend to be fresh. You can see and taste the freshness; the kernels are plump, not withered, and the color is clear and, well, nutty. Because they perish quickly, nuts and seeds should be stored in the refrigerator or freezer in warmer-than-temperate climates.

So here it is — a parade of meatless entrées designed to satisfy the palate, nourish the body, and harm not a soul. I savor these clear, vegetarian nights.

Spinach Lasagna

This recipe was created especially for simplicity's sake. I often serve it when kitchen time is somewhat limited, yet I want a substantial, satisfying dish. My favorite part of the recipe is not having to cook the lasagna noodles; they cook to perfection while the casserole bakes.

For the Sauce:

¼ cup olive oil

1 chopped onion

2 cloves garlic

½ cup TVP (textured vegetable protein, available in natural food stores)

¾ cup hot water

1 tablespoon soy sauce

1 28-ounce jar tomato sauce (such as Ragu)

1 6-ounce can tomato paste

1¼ cups dry red wine

1 cup water

1 tablespoon basil leaves

1 tablespoon oregano leaves

For the Filling:

1 10-ounce package frozen chopped, spinach, thawed

2 cups ricotta cheese

¾ cup Parmesan cheese, divided

2 beaten eggs

⅛ teaspoon nutmeg

Additional ingredients:

8 ounces lasagna noodles

1 pound mozzarella cheese

To make the sauce, heat the olive oil in a large saucepan; in it, sauté the onion and garlic. While they cook, pour the hot water and soy sauce over the TVP in a small bowl. Let it soak 5 minutes, then add it to the onion. Cook 2 minutes, then add the tomato sauce, tomato paste, wine, water, basil and oregano. Let the sauce simmer gently; stir it frequently while you prepare the filling.

For the filling, squeeze moisture from the thawed spinach, and combine it in a bowl with the ricotta, ½ cup of the Parmesan, the eggs, and the nutmeg. Mix well.

Grate the mozzarella cheese. Rinse the lasagna noodles under cold water, one by one. (This rinses off excess starch which is usually removed in boiling.) Preheat the oven to 350 degrees. Now you're ready to assemble the lasagna. Use a deep 9-inch by 13-inch baking dish.

Layer as follows: ⅓ of the sauce; half the noodles; ⅓ of the sauce; half the mozzarella; all the filling; ⅓ of the sauce; remaining lasagna noodles; ⅓ of the sauce; remaining mozzarella cheese; remaining sauce; sprinkle with remaining ¼ cup Parmesan.

Bake uncovered 60 minutes. Let stand 10 minutes before serving.

Yields 12 pieces

Variation: For a delicious, dairy-free version, make the following changes:
- substitute 2 cups mashed, firm tofu plus ½ teaspoon seasoned salt for the ricotta cheese
- omit the Parmesan cheese
- substitute soy mozzarella for dairy mozzarella

Chile Relleno Cornbread

Rich and satisfying, yet light and spicy, this unusual cornbread is not a side dish, but an entrée.

2 7-ounce cans whole green chiles
4 ounces Monterey Jack cheese (or soy Jack)
4 ounces cheddar cheese (or soy cheese), grated
I cup chopped onion
½ cup chopped sweet red pepper
½ cup chopped green pepper
I cup corn kernels
1¼ cup buttermilk (or soymilk, soured with a tablespoon lemon juice)
½ cup mild oil, such as canola, or melted butter
3 eggs, beaten
I tablespoon honey
1½ cups cornmeal
1½ teaspoons baking powder
¾ teaspoon baking soda
I teaspoon salt
I teaspoon cumin
I teaspoon chili powder

Cut the Jack cheese into "fingers" to fit inside the chiles, and put them in; reserve. Grate the cheddar and keep it separate.

Chop the onion and peppers; combine with corn.

Combine the buttermilk, oil, beaten eggs and honey; mix well.

Preheat oven to 375 degrees. Combine all the dry ingredients, sifting the baking soda as it's added; mix well.

Butter an 8-inch by 12-inch baking pan thoroughly. Add liquid to dry ingredients and mix well; do not beat. Stir in the chopped vegetables. Spoon the batter into the buttered pan. Arrange the stuffed chiles in the batter, pressing them into place firmly. Sprinkle the grated cheese around the chiles.

Bake until firm and lightly browned, 30 to 40 minutes. Do not overbake.

Yield: 8 servings

SUGGESTED MENU
Chips, Guacamole, and Salsa
Chile Relleno Cornbread
Mexican Rice Salad
Tossed Green Salad
Coconut-Tapioca Pudding

Nut-Meat Loaf

This is the dish to serve friends or relatives who believe they can't make it through the day without their ration of meat. It's also the dish for anyone who loves a hearty, old-fashioned meal. When I serve Nut-Meat Loaf with mashed potatoes, a green salad, and an ear of corn, it takes me right back to the '50s.

1 cup cooked brown rice
2 cups grated cheddar cheese
½ cup wheat germ
½ cup fresh bread crumbs
1 cup chopped (or processed) walnuts
1 cup chopped (or processed) mushrooms
1 cup finely chopped onion
½ cup grated carrot
½ cup minced green pepper
5 beaten eggs
2 tablespoons soy sauce
2 tablespoons Dijon mustard
½ teaspoon each black pepper, thyme, marjoram, and sage

Prepare all ingredients, placing them in a large mixing bowl. Mix thoroughly with clean hands or a wooden spoon.

Preheat oven to 350 degrees. Butter a 9-inch square baking pan and press loaf mixture in evenly. Bake 50 to 60 minutes, until firm. Serve hot from the pan topped with Irresistible Mushrooms (page 99).

Yield: 6 servings

Spinach Nutloaf or Nutburgers

Spinach Nutloaf is based on rice and spinach, with nuts, seeds, egg, and cheese added to provide full-bodied flavor and a full dose of protein. This entrée satisfies meat-and-potato lovers with its bold flavor and hearty texture.

For burgers, just shape the loaf mixture into patties and fry them on a hot, oiled griddle or pan. Spinach Nutburgers are fabulous on whole wheat buns with a thin slice of sweet onion, lettuce, and tomato.

2¼ cups cooked brown rice
⅓ cup ground walnuts
⅓ cup ground sunflower seeds
⅓ cup ground cashew nuts
20 ounces frozen, chopped, spinach, thawed and squeezed dry
2 large eggs
¼ cup soy sauce
½ a medium onion, chopped finely
1½ cups grated raw cheddar cheese

Grind the nuts and seeds in a blender, food processor, or rotary hand grater until they are finely chopped, about the consistency of very coarse flour. Combine with all other ingredients, blending thoroughly with clean hands.

For the Nutloaf: Press the mixture into a well buttered 8-inch square pan. Bake 35 to 40 minutes, until firm, at 350 degrees. Serve hot.

For the Nutburgers: Shape the mixture into 6 to 8 patties and fry until brown. Let them cook at least 10 minutes on the first side, so they hold together when turned over.

Yield: 4 to 6 servings
(9 squares of loaf or 6 to 8 burgers)

Mushroom Burgers

Taste these juicy burgers once and you'll make them often. They're especially quick and easy to put together with the help of a food processor. The onions, mushrooms, bread slices, walnuts, and parsley are prepped in a matter of minutes. Add cooked rice, eggs, and spices, then shape and fry the burgers.

½ pound mushrooms

½ a medium onion (½ cup chopped)

3 to 4 slices hearty whole wheat bread (to make 1⅔ cups crumbs)

¾ cup walnuts

⅓ cup finely chopped parsley

1 tablespoon sesame seeds

1 clove pressed garlic

1 cup cooked brown rice

2 eggs

1 teaspoon powdered sage

1 tablespoon soy sauce

¾ teaspoon salt (or to taste)

Wash and dry the mushrooms. If you have a food processor, use the blade to chop them finely. Put them in a bowl, and continue processing with the blade; chop the onions finely; make crumbs of the bread; chop the walnuts (not too finely) and mince the parsley. (Or chop the vegetables by hand.)

Start heating the griddle or a heavyweight frying pan. Add the sesame seeds, garlic, rice, eggs, sage, soy sauce, and salt to the bowl; mix well. Form 8 burgers.

Heat a small amount of oil on the griddle or hot pan; sauté the burgers until nicely browned, 5 to 8 minutes per side.

Serve Mushroom Burgers on buns with whatever trimmings you like, or plain, or with your sauce of choice.

Yield: 8 servings

Grilled Tofu

This is the way I cook tofu most often, either to be eaten hot off the grill, or for use in another preparation. Grilled tofu is firmer than raw tofu, and tastier. It's perfect for use in stir-fries because it doesn't fall apart.

1½ pounds firm tofu
½ cup soy sauce
1 tablespoon mild oil, such as
    canola

Cut the tofu into ½-inch slabs. Pour the soy sauce into an 8-inch by 12-inch baking dish, and lay the tofu slabs in it to marinate. You may wish to add pressed garlic or grated ginger to the marinade; it's good with both. A pinch of curry powder is also good.

Heat the griddle over low heat for 5 to 10 minutes, then increase the heat to medium-high and pour on the oil, distributing it evenly on the griddle with a spatula.

Remove the tofu from its marinade, shake it slightly to remove any excess, and place it on the hot grill. It'll spatter a bit, then calm down. Reserve excess marinade, about ¼ cup, in the refrigerator, for another cooking project; use within one week.

Grill the tofu until golden (7 to 10 minutes), then flip to cook the other side until it's golden too.

Yield: 4 servings

Cashew Vegetable Curry

Choose either cashew milk or coconut milk for the sauce — both are delicious; the coconut milk version is more delicate, creamy, and rich.

For the Sauce:

- **1 cup diced onion**
- **4 cloves pressed garlic**
- **2 teaspoons finely grated ginger**
- **⅓ cup water**
- **1 tablespoon fine quality curry powder**
- **1 tablespoon ground sage**
- **2 teaspoons paprika**
- **1 tablespoon seasoned salt**
- **1 teaspoon black pepper**
- **½ cup tomato paste**
- **1 cup raw cashew nuts and 3 cups water (or 1¾ cups coconut milk and 1¾ cups plain soymilk or milk)**

For the Rest:

- **1 pound firm or regular tofu, drained and towel-dried**
- **⅓ cup soy sauce**
- **½ cup raw cashew nuts**
- **2 medium yams (3 cups roll-cut pieces)**
- **1 tablespoon mild oil**
- **1 medium head broccoli (2 cups chopped)**
- **4 small zucchini (1-inch diameter, 5 inches long), roll-cut**
- **2 tablespoons butter**
- **½ pound mushrooms, washed and halved**
- **1 sweet red pepper, diced**

Cut the tofu in ¾-inch slabs and marinate it in the soy sauce about 10 minutes, turning once.

If you're using the cashew milk base, blenderize 1 cup of cashews with 3 cups water until smooth, about 5 minutes.

For the sauce, sauté the onion, garlic, and ginger in the ⅓ cup water until onion is transparent (add water if necessary), then add the curry, sage, paprika, and seasoned salt. Cook 2 minutes, then stir in the black pepper and the tomato paste. Mix well.

Add cashew mixture or the coconut milk/soymilk. Whisk and set over low heat to cook 10 minutes.

Grill the slabs of tofu until browned on both sides. When they're done, cut them in 1-inch squares.

Toast the ½ cup cashews in an unpreheated toaster oven, about 12 minutes at 300 degrees.

Prepare all the vegetables. Start the yams cooking in a bit of hot water in a hot wok. Cover the wok, stirring frequently, and cook yams until they're soft, but not falling apart. Remove them to a bowl and cover it.

Heat the 1 tablespoon oil in the wok, and toss in the broccoli and zucchini. Over high heat, stir-fry them until barely tender, about 4 minutes. Remove them to the bowl with the yams; cover it halfway. (If fully covered, the broccoli may turn drab green.)

Melt the butter in the wok, and toss in the mushrooms; stir-fry briefly until they're half tender; add the red pepper and cook a minute or two more, until the mushrooms are done. Now put all the cooked vegetables back in the wok. Add the tofu and the sauce, and season to taste with salt and cayenne pepper. Stir in half the toasted cashews.

Let the curry simmer for a few minutes, then serve over steaming couscous or hot basmati rice. Garnish with the remaining cashews.

Yield: 6 to 8 servings

Tofu Patties

A favorite recipe, Tofu Patties have been on my menu for at least ten years. They're perfect with rice and stir-fried vegetables.

In this recipe, the results depend upon the freshness and the texture of the tofu. It must be very fresh and medium-firm (what we call "regular" tofu on Maui). Firm tofu may be used instead of regular, but the patties will be less delicate. Don't try making this with soft tofu, though; the patties won't hold together. Before mashing it, I wrap the tofu in a clean terrycloth towel to draw out the excess moisture. Serve Tofu Patties topped with Chinese Brown Sauce, (page 66).

3½ cups mashed medium-firm tofu, towel-dried

3 beaten eggs

2 teaspoons aluminum-free baking powder

1 teaspoon salt

2 tablespoons wheat germ

¼ cup grated carrot (medium grate)

2 tablespoons minced parsley or Chinese parsley

½ cup minced green onion

Oil for frying (just a bit)

Towel-dry and mash the tofu with a potato masher. Beat the eggs and add them, along with the baking powder, salt, wheat germ, carrot, parsley, and green onion.

Heat a griddle or a couple of frying pans, and add a little oil to cover the bottom of the pan. Form patties with a 2½-inch diameter, about ½-inch thick. When the oil is hot, fry the patties over medium heat until golden, about 5 minutes per side. Turn only once.

These are best served immediately, but you can store the first ones in the oven, uncovered, at 250 degrees, while you fry the rest. Allow 2 to 3 patties per person, depending on what else is served.

Yield: 4 to 6 servings

Tofu Croutons

For ease of preparation and radical tofu transformation, this recipe works wonders. Tofu croutons taste good, and they don't fall apart. People eat astounding amounts of these, especially if left uncovered on the counter when they come out of the oven.

1 scant pound tofu, regular or firm (not soft)

¼ cup soy sauce

1 tablespoon extra virgin-olive oil

¼ teaspoon paprika

Drain the tofu in a strainer for at least 5 minutes, then dry it thoroughly with a clean towel. Cut it into cubes 1-inch square by ¾-inch thick.

Combine soy sauce, olive oil, and paprika in an 8-inch square baking pan, Add the cubed tofu. Bake 30 minutes at 350 degrees, then 25 minutes more at 375 degrees. Turn the cubes after about 40 minutes of baking.

When it's done, all the liquid in the pan will have evaporated, and the tofu will have a golden crust.

Yield: 4 servings when combined with vegetables

Cauliflower-Cheese Enchiladas

Why would anyone in her right mind put cauliflower in enchiladas? Good question. The answer is that it lends body to the enchilada filling without being heavy or strongly flavored in itself.

You see, I love enchiladas, and I like to be able to eat a couple of them, along with salad, rice and beans, and maybe even a piece of Carrot Poppyseed Bundt Cake for dessert (page 138). But regular enchiladas (those filled with lots of cheese) leave me too full to enjoy the whole fiesta, and still be able to dance afterwards. So I invented these. And guess what? No one — not one person — has been able to identify the cauliflower.

For the Filling:
1 small, firm cauliflower (to yield 2¼ cups, chopped)
1 7-ounce can chopped green chiles
2 cups (½ pound) grated Monterey Jack cheese (or soy cheese)
⅓ cup minced onion
½ teaspoon salt
½ teaspoon ground cumin
¾ cup tofu sour cream (page 67) or sour cream
24 ripe black olives (pitted)

For the Enchiladas:
12 corn tortillas (5 to 6 inches in diameter)
1 10-ounce can enchilada sauce

For the Garnish:
1 recipe Avocado Dip (page 56)
½ sweet red pepper, chopped finely
⅓ cup chopped Chinese parsley

Coarsely chop and steam the cauliflower until tender, 12 to 15 minutes. Cool it, then chop it very finely.

Combine all filling ingredients except olives. Mix well. Preheat oven to 350 degrees.

Pour about ⅓ of the can of enchilada sauce into a 9 or 10-inch by 13-inch baking pan and tilt the pan to coat the bottom with sauce. Pour the remaining sauce into a pie plate. Dip the tortillas, one by one into the sauce in the pie plate; shake off excess sauce; scoop rounded ¼-cupfuls of filling into a log shape across the middle of the tortilla. Put 2 olives inside, then roll the tortilla around the filling. Place seam down in the baking pan. When all the enchiladas are rolled, there should be a bit of sauce left in the pie pan; drizzle it atop the enchiladas. (Note: these are not swimming in sauce, like traditional enchiladas.)

Cover the pan with foil and bake 30 minutes. Serve immediately, garnished with Avocado Dip, Chinese parsley, and red peppers.

Yield: 6 servings of 2 enchiladas apiece

> **Sometimes corn tortillas are too dry to bend, and they break instead. If that happens, wrap a pile of them securely in foil, and warm them in the oven or toaster oven until they soften (about 8 to 10 minutes) at 350 degrees.**

Curried Tofu and Green Beans with Basil

Since neither chopping beans nor grilling cubed tofu proceeds quicky, this is a dish to make when you have plenty of time or a friendly pair of hands to help.

For the Curry:

1 pound firm tofu

¼ cup soy sauce

1 pound green beans

1 pound butternut squash or pumpkin squash

For the Sauce:

1½ tablespoons butter

1 tablespoon mild oil, such as canola

1½ teaspoons brown mustard seed

1½ teaspoons ground coriander seed

1½ teaspoons ground cumin seed

1½ teaspoons turmeric

1½ teaspoons finely grated fresh ginger root

1¼ teaspoons salt

3½ tablespoons tomato paste

2½ cups vegetable bouillon

3 tablespoons lemon juice

1½ tablespoons soy sauce

1½ teaspoons honey

2¼ tablespoons cornstarch or 1½ tablespoons kuzu, dissolved in 3 tablespoons water

½ cup fresh basil leaves packed, thinly sliced

For the Garnish:

1 tomato

½ cup Chinese parsley

1 lime

Drain and towel-dry the tofu; cut it in ¾-inch cubes. Marinate the tofu 20 minutes in the ¼ cup soy sauce, turning to saturate it on all sides.

While the tofu marinates, combine the mustard, coriander, cumin, turmeric, ginger, and salt in a small bowl. Also, prepare the bouillon; squeeze lemon for juice; dissolve the cornstarch or kuzu in the 3 tablespoons water and reserve; slice basil leaves; and prepare garnish ingredients: finely cube the tomato, chop the Chinese parsley, and cut the lime into wedges, removing seeds.

Grill the marinated tofu on a hot, lightly oiled griddle or nonstick pan. Turn the cubes every 2 to 3 minutes, to grill each side. Keep hot.

Wash and trim the beans; cut them on the diagonal in 1½-inch pieces. Seed and peel the squash; cut it in ¾-inch cubes. Put the squash in a steamer over boiling water, reduce heat to a simmer. After 10 minutes add the green beans; and cook 10 more minutes.

While the vegetables steam, make the sauce. Heat the butter and oil in a frying pan. Add the spices and mix well; sauté 2 minutes, then mix in the tomato paste, adding hot bouillon. When blended, add lemon juice, soy sauce, honey, and basil. Let it all simmer together while you place the steamed vegetables and the tofu on a deep serving platter. Keep them covered and hot. Add the dissolved thickener to the sauce, and when it thickens, pour it over the tofu and vegetables. Garnish the platter with tomato, Chinese parsley, and lime wedges.

Yield: 4 to 5 servings

I bought a new
salad bowl yester-
day. Today I
rubbed it with miner-
al oil and left it dry-
ing on the counter.
Not really drying;
it's sitting there
absorbing the oil.

Italian Tofu Steak

These succulent "steaks" are assembled in less than 5 minutes. Bake sweet potatoes or yams alongside them, and serve with a fresh green salad for a nearly effortless preparation. Leftovers make excellent sandwich filling, especially on toasted sourdough with mustard, lettuce, and a slice of tomato.

¼ cup soy sauce

7 tablespoons soymilk or milk

1½ pounds firm tofu, sliced in ½-inch slabs

2 tablespoons nutritional yeast flakes (optional)

1¼ teaspoons paprika

¾ teaspoon poultry seasoning (optional)

2 scant teaspoons oregano leaf

Preheat oven to 350 degrees. Combine soy sauce and soymilk in an 8-inch by 12-inch baking pan. Arrange the sliced tofu evenly in pan, making sure the marinade has thoroughly doused it.

Sprinkle the surface of the tofu evenly with nutritional yeast and seasonings; bake 40 minutes. The liquid should evaporate completely. Check the tofu after 30 minutes, so if your oven runs hot, it doesn't burn. When the liquid is gone, serve immediately.

Yield: 4 to 6 servings

Tofu Mock Chicken and Gravy

This was a Maui favorite during the '80s, when eating nutritional yeast was considered "the vegetarian solution." Because of its high protein and B vitamin content, lots of us sprinkled yeast on our salads, our popcorn, and our tofu (that is to say, on just about everything we ate).

Later we learned what we never wanted to believe, that there can be Too Much of a Good Thing. Like all concentrated foods, yeast is valuable in moderation. In excess, it can lead to food sensitivities and allergies.

Here's a recipe that shows off its use as a flavor enhancer for tofu. And it does taste remarkably like chicken.

For the Tofu:

1½ pound firm or regular tofu
¼ cup soy sauce
¼ cup wheat germ
¼ cup nutritional yeast
¼ teaspoon seasoned salt
¼ teaspoon powdered sage
¼ teaspoon thyme
2 tablespoons oil (or less; just enough to coat the frying pan)

For the Gravy:

1 onion
1 tablespoon mild oil
¼ cup nutritional yeast
¼ cup raw tahini (sesame butter)
1 tablespoon garbanzo bean flour
1 tablespoon soy sauce
1 to 1¼ cups water
Salt and pepper to taste
2 tablespoons minced parsley

Towel-dry the tofu and cut it in two on the diagonal. Lay the halves on the cut edge, then cut half-inch triangular slices. Pour the soy sauce onto a baking tray large enough to accommodate the tofu, and let it marinate for 15 minutes, turning once.

Mix the wheat germ, the ¼ cup yeast, the seasoned salt, sage, and thyme on a plate. Heat a griddle, nonstick pan, or skillet until it's hot, then add oil just to coat it. The amount will depend on the size and type of pan.

When the oil is hot, dredge the tofu in the yeast mixture, and fry it until golden, turning once. This takes 10 to 15 minutes. While the tofu is cooking, make the gravy.

Sauté the onion in hot oil in a skillet until it is transparent. Blenderize the yeast, tahini, flour, soy sauce, and 1 cup of water. Add blender mixture to the cooked onion and stir well; cook for 10 minutes, adding the additional ¼ cup water, salt, and pepper as desired.

Serve the tofu on a platter in a single layer doused with sauce. Garnish with minced parsley.

Yield: 4 to 6 servings

SUGGESTED MENU
Tofu Mock Chicken and Gravy
Memorable Mashed Potatoes
(make an extra recipe of gravy for the potatoes)
Tossed Green Salad with Tomatoes
Corn on the Cob

Tofu Parmesan

It's easy to put this layered casserole together once the three components are prepared; just bread and fry the tofu, grate the cheese, and sauté the mushrooms. Then layer and bake. The casserole may be assembled in advance, refrigerated, and baked the next day.

1½ pounds firm tofu, towel-dried

⅓ cup soy sauce

Cornmeal for breading tofu and oil for frying it

2 cups tomato sauce, from a jar

1⅓ cups grated mozzarella cheese or soy cheese (about ⅓ pound)

4 cups sliced mushrooms (about ¾ pound)

3 tablespoons butter

⅓ cup Parmesan cheese

Cut the tofu in ½-inch thick slices and lay it out in a pan containing the soy sauce allowing it to marinate at least 10 minutes, turning once.

While the tofu marinates, grate the cheese and slice the mushrooms. Melt the butter and sauté the mushrooms until barely tender; they should not release their juices. Reserve.

Heat a griddle or a couple of frying pans for the tofu, and add as little oil as possible for frying. Blot excess soy sauce from tofu and dredge it in cornmeal. Heat the oil until hot but not smoking, and place the tofu in the pan. Fry about 7 minutes per side, until golden, over medium heat.

Use a 9-inch square baking pan for the casserole. To assemble, make layers as follows:

¾ cup tomato sauce

½ the fried tofu

½ the grated cheese

½ the mushrooms

Repeat layers, then top with remaining ½ cup sauce, and the Parmesan. Bake until hot and bubbly, 20 to 25 minutes at 350 degrees, uncovered.

Yield: 4 to 6 servings

Nepalese Vegetable Curry

Nepalese curries are rich in spices and vegetables, but not in butter, cream, or coconut milk. They are what we call "thin" curries, but don't misunderstand; while the sauce is thin, not creamy, it is nonetheless full of flavor, and excellent over rice. To my taste (and waist), it's the best curry of all.

4 cups peeled and cubed butternut squash

1 medium onion

2 cups chopped Japanese (long) eggplant

2 tablespoons butter

1 teaspoon whole cumin seed

1 teaspoon turmeric

1 teaspoon ground coriander seed

1 teaspoon garam masala (a spice blend found in Indian markets)

1½ tablespoon peeled and finely grated fresh ginger

1 red or green hot chile pepper (optional)

6 large cloves pressed garlic

2 tablespoons mild oil, such as canola

1 14-ounce can whole, peeled tomatoes, chopped or squashed

1 bunch fresh spinach (6 cups very coarsely chopped)

1 teaspoon salt

1 cup cooked kidney beans (canned or bottled are fine)

1 to 2 tablespoons soy sauce (to taste)

First, steam the squash (about 15 minutes). Cut the onion into thin half-moons. Cut the eggplant lengthwise, then into ½-inch chunks.

Heat the butter in a heavy skillet, and fry the spices, ginger, chile, and garlic. Cook a minute, then add the onion and the oil. Stir-fry 2 minutes, then add the eggplant. Stir-fry 5 minutes over medium heat.

Add the tomatoes with their liquid. Cover the pan and reduce the heat to a simmer. Wash the spinach meticulously, so no grit remains. When the eggplant is nearly done, add the steamed butternut, the salt, the kidney beans, and the soy sauce to the pan. Lay the spinach over all. Cover and cook until it is tender, about 5 minutes. Mix well and serve immediately over brown rice.

Yield: 4 to 6 servings

Refried Beans

Refried beans, affectionately known as refries, are used in Mexican cooking both as a side dish and as a filling for burritos. Pinto beans are always used for making refries in traditional Mexican cookery; their bland flavor is a perfect backdrop for the pungent tastes of onion, garlic, and chilies.

The refries recipe below is different from most. Here, the beans are never fried. Spices (rather than frying in fat) provide the base of flavor, with olive oil added as an option at the end, where its delicate taste and nutritional value are not compromised by high heat.

1½ cups pinto beans
1 small onion, chopped
2 to 4 large cloves pressed garlic
½ cup of reserved bean cooking water
2 tablespoons chili powder
About 1 teaspoon salt
1 tablespoon extra-virgin olive oil (optional)

Pick through the beans for stones and foreign matter, then soak them for at least 6 hours, preferably overnight. Soaking water must cover beans by at least 4 inches. Drain and rinse beans after soaking, then cover with fresh water by 2 inches.

Simmer the beans until tender, about 2 hours, or pressure cook 20 minutes. Drain the cooked beans, reserving the cooking water.

In a large, heavy skillet, "fry" the onion and garlic in ¼ cup of the bean cooking water. When the onions are transparent, add the cooked beans and a bit more cooking water. Using a potato masher, mash the beans thoroughly, adding spices, salt to taste, and additional liquid as desired. This can be done while the beans are still cooking over low heat.

Two things are happening in the pan. The beans are absorbing liquid greedily, and liquid is also evaporating over the heat. At this time, consider the texture you'd like for the dish you're preparing. If it's a side dish, be generous with the liquid. If it's for filling burritos immediately (without cooling), add the liquid cautiously; too much makes the job messy and difficult. If the beans are to be used for filling later, you have more leeway because they stiffen as they cool.

When the beans are seasoned and textured as desired, turn off the heat and stir in the olive oil.

Yield: about 9 side-dish servings, or filling for 10 burritos

Bean, Cheese, and Chile Burritos

Burritos are easy to eat out-of-hand, but they're even better under a bubbling enchilada sauce and a layer of melted cheese. These are filled with refried beans, grated Monterey Jack cheese and a spoonful of Green Chile Pesto (page 69).

6 whole wheat tortillas

⅔ recipe Refried Beans, (page 125) or 2 cups canned refries

1 cup grated Monterey Jack cheese or soy cheese (or more, to taste)

½ small, sweet onion, minced

6 tablespoons Green Chile Pesto (optional but recommended)

1 10-ounce can enchilada sauce and cheese for the top (optional)

Wrap tortillas tightly in foil and bake 10 minutes at 350 degrees, to make them flexible enough to roll without breaking. (If they're already pliable, skip this step.)

Lay out all the tortillas, and on each, place ¼ to ⅓ cup beans in the form of a flattened log, just below the middle. Evenly sprinkle cheese, onion, and a tablespoon of Green Chile Pesto over the beans. Fold sides in over ends of filling, envelope-style, then roll the tortillas up.

Place on a heat-proof platter and douse with enchilada sauce and cheese if desired. Cover, and bake briefly, about 15 minutes at 400 degrees, until hot. For crisp burritos, omit sauce, brush with melted butter, and bake uncovered 15 to 20 minutes.

Yield: 6 burritos

Lentil Nutloaf

Vegan food (food containing no animal products) has become quite popular on Maui. It can be tricky to prepare, though, because eggs are hard to replace as a binding agent.

In this recipe cornstarch and whole wheat flour may be used instead of eggs to bind the grated beets, walnuts, lentils, and rice. The loaf is tasty. Be forewarned though — the beets give this loaf a "rare" look that may cause double-takes at the table.

1 rounded cup brown lentils
½ cup minced onion
1 cup finely chopped walnuts
6 cloves pressed garlic
2 cups finely grated beet, well-drained in a strainer
½ cup chopped green pepper
1¼ cups cooked rice (leftovers are fine)
⅓ cup wheat germ
1½ teaspoons dried basil leaves
1½ tablespoons seasoned salt
⅓ cup olive oil
2 tablespoons cornstarch
2 tablespoons whole wheat flour
1 tablespoon balsamic vinegar

Cook the lentils until tender in boiling, unsalted water for 35 minutes. When the lentils are done, preheat the oven to 350 degrees. Drain the lentils well, pressing excess moisture out of them. This will prevent a mushy loaf. Mix them thoroughly with all the remaining ingredients. Cornstarch and whole wheat flour can be replaced with 2 eggs, if desired. Generously oil an 8-inch square baking pan and press in the lentil mixture evenly. Bake 45 minutes, uncovered.

Serve Lentil Nutloaf with a creamy sauce like Béchamel Nouvelle (page 63), a fresh salad, baked squash, and Cornbread (page 171).

Yield: 4 to 6 servings

Moroccan Pepper-Lentil Stew
Over Couscous

I was eighteen when I first landed in Casablanca, and was captivated by the foods and the marketplace. In the center of old Moroccan towns, vendors sell their wares in outdoor suks, or stalls. Some of them sell nothing but spices. One day I found a bright-eyed old man who had huge burlap bags of spices. I kept repeating that I wanted the ones I could use to make Moroccan food when I got home. The packets he sold me contained paprika, ginger, chili, and cumin — and the combination worked.

I round eggplant (about 12 ounces)

I to 2 tablespoons olive oil

Salt

I cup brown lentils

3 cups water

I onion

4 cloves garlic

I small, hot pepper (optional but recommended for authenticity)

I tablespoon extra-virgin olive oil

2 to 3 medium carrots (to make I cup, roll-cut)

I large green pepper

I large red bell pepper

4 to 6 Roma* tomatoes, fresh or canned (to make 1½ cups chopped)

2 tablespoons soy sauce

⅔ cup water

2 teaspoons paprika

½ teaspoon ground ginger

I teaspoon chili powder

1½ teaspoons ground cumin seed

I teaspoon salt

½ cup pitted, chopped Kalamata olives

2 cups couscous

2 teaspoons salt

2 to 4 tablespoons butter (optional)

2 cups boiling water

Preheat oven to 400 degrees. Slice the eggplant into ½-inch thick rounds, brush them with olive oil and sprinkle lightly with salt on both sides. Place them on a cookie sheet and bake on the lowest oven racks until tender, about 10 minutes per side.

Bring the lentils and water to a boil, reduce heat to a simmer and cover. Simmer 20 minutes.

While the eggplant bakes and the lentils simmer, chop the onion, garlic, and hot pepper. Sauté them in a pot over low heat in the olive oil for 5 minutes, then add the carrots. Cook uncovered over low heat 10 minutes.

Dice the peppers into bite-size chunks and the tomatoes finely. (*I suggest using Roma tomatoes, which are the oblong, Italian type, as they are meatier and less juicy than table tomatoes and are good for cooking because they don't add liquid to the dish.) Add them to the pot along with the soy sauce, water, paprika, ginger, chili powder, cumin, and salt. When they're done, add the cooked lentils and their water; increase the heat until the pot simmers. Chop the eggplant and prepare the olives; add them to the stew and simmer gently, uncovered.

To make couscous, place it in a deep bowl with the salt and butter, if desired. Add the boiling water, stir once, and cover tightly. Let rest 5 minutes. Fluff it up and serve, topped with stew.

Yield: 5 servings

Dal Bata

This fragrant and delicious dal *or stew is thick but not heavy. For an everyday meal, it's good over brown basmati rice with chapatis and a tossed salad. For a more festive Indian meal, add Curried Vegetables (page 105) and Banana Chutney (page 60) to the menu.*

1½ cups red lentils

4½ cups water

3 cloves pressed garlic

3½ cups peeled, cubed pumpkin

2 cups chopped potatoes

1 to 2 teaspoons salt (to taste)

1 finely diced onion

1 teaspoon brown mustard seeds

1 tablespoon butter

1 tablespoon mild oil, such as canola

1 teaspoon quality curry powder

1 teaspoon quality chili powder

1 teaspoon sage

¼ teaspoon ginger powder

1 to 2 tablespoons soy sauce

1 cup frozen green peas, thawed

Cayenne pepper to taste

Rinse the lentils thoroughly, until the water runs clear. Place in a pot with the water and garlic. Boil, then reduce heat and simmer 15 minutes. Add pumpkin, potatoes, and salt; simmer 15 minutes more. If you prefer the dal thick, cook it without a cover.

Separately, sauté onion and mustard seeds in a mixture of butter and oil. When the onions are transparent, add the curry, chili powder, sage, and ginger. Mix well, adding a bit of water if necessary to prevent sticking; cook spices for a minute or two with the onions, then add this mixture to the lentil pot. Use a rubber scraper to clean pan thoroughly.

Add 1 tablespoon soy sauce and the peas. Heat through. Check the seasoning, adding soy sauce or salt to taste. Serve immediately, while the peas are bright green. (The dal will be equally good on the second day, even if the peas do turn drab.)

Yield: 6 to 8 servings

Stuffed Pumpkin Squash

This is a merry platter to serve. The pumpkin is not only stuffed, but overstuffed, so the hat sits atop the savory filling an inch or so above its rotund base. It looks like the pumpkin is doffing its hat.

1 3-pound pumpkin squash
2 cups cooked brown rice
1 cup fresh whole wheat bread
    crumbs
⅔ cup toasted seeds — a mixture
    of sunflower, pumpkin,
    and sesame
½ cup minced onion
½ cup chopped celery, cranberries,
    or olives (optional)
1 cup grated cheese or soy cheese
    (I use lowfat mozzarella)
1 teaspoon basil
½ teaspoon sage
½ teaspoon dry mustard
⅛ teaspoon nutmeg
½ cup minced parsley
1½ tablespoons soy sauce
2 tablespoons port wine
    (or sherry)
1 tablespoon extra-virgin olive oil

Cut the top off the pumpkin attractively. Remove seeds and strings. Preheat oven to 375 degrees.

Combine remaining ingredients. Mix well, and pack the mixture into and on top of the pumpkin; smooth it, and place the top over all. Place the pumpkin on a flat baking tray and bake 75 to 90 minutes, until the pumpkin is easily pierced with a sharp knife. Serve immediately, with Chinese Brown Sauce (page 66), if desired.

Yield: 4 servings

> SUGGESTED MENU
> **Homestyle Mushroom Soup**
> **Stuffed Pumpkin Squash with Chinese Brown Sauce**
> **Tossed Green Salad**
> **Holiday Fruit Bars**

Delicata Mexicana

Simple to make and highly unusual, this dish is a combination of chiles rellenos and stuffed, baked squash. You fill a couple of green chiles with cheese (or soy cheese) and place them, along with some salsa, in a Delicata squash half. Then you bake it. Garnish each serving with guacamole, salsa, and sour cream, if you like, and a festive little Mexican boat is the end result. The slightly sweet taste of the squash is wonderful with the richness of cheese and the heat of the chiles. Serve with Spicy Fried Rice (page 84), Refried Beans (page 125), and a green salad for a great — and easy — meal.

3 Delicata squash, 1½ to 2 pounds each

2 7-ounce cans whole green chiles

12 ounces pepper Jack cheese (or pepper soy cheese)

12 ounces fresh salsa

1 recipe Avocado Dip (page 56)

Sour cream (optional)

Important: The squash must be cut in half lengthwise without cutting off either of the ends, because the ends must be intact to hold everything in. Scoop out the seeds. Preheat the oven to 350 degrees.

Salt the squash lightly. Open the cans of chiles, and cut a tapered "finger" of cheese to fit into each chile. Place the filled chiles in the squash halves and spoon a bit of salsa around them.

Place the filled squash in a lightly oiled baking dish and cover it tightly. Bake 45 minutes at 350 degrees, then increase oven heat to 375 for 15 minutes. The squash is done when it is easily pierced with a fork.

Place the squashes on their individual serving plates and garnish attractively with the guacamole, salsa, and optional sour cream. Add rice, beans, and salad to each plate, and serve.

Yield: 6 servings

Chop Suey

This dish tastes remarkably like the chop suey I loved as a teenager in the San Fernando Valley, where I was first enamored of Chinese food.

Two options are offered for adding protein to this popular vegetable entrée. Choose either tamari almonds or fried tempeh, whichever suits your mood and menu. Serve over steaming rice.

For the Sauce:

2 cups vegetable bouillon

2½ tablespoons soy sauce

1 teaspoon honey

4 teaspoons rice vinegar

2 tablespoons cornstarch or 3 tablespoons kuzu

2½ tablespoons sherry

For the Vegetables:

1 tablespoon mild oil, such as canola

4 cups chopped broccoli (2 small heads)

1½ cups celery (3 stalks), sliced on the diagonal

7 cups bok choy (1 small bunch), stems sliced on the diagonal, leaves sliced thinly (keep leaves and stems separate)

2 cloves pressed garlic

2 cups sliced mushrooms

1 5-ounce can sliced bamboo shoots, rinsed and drained

10 ounces fresh bean sprouts

For the Options (choose one):

½ cup tamari almonds*
or 8 ounces tempeh, prepared as for Indonesian Tempeh and Vegetables (page 133, steps 3 and 4)

For the sauce, heat the bouillon, soy sauce, honey, and vinegar in a small saucepan. Separately, combine the thickener and the sherry; set aside.

Prepare the tempeh, if you've selected that option. Prep all the vegetables.

Place a wok or very large skillet over medium-high heat for a minute or two; add the oil and let it heat up. Toss in the broccoli, celery, bok choy stems, and the garlic; stir-fry about 5 minutes, until everything is hot and starting to cook. Add the mushrooms and bamboo shoots and continue stir-frying for 3 minutes, until they have started to cook too. Now add the bean sprouts, the bok choy leaves, and the tempeh, if you're using it; stir them in well, and cook for one more minute.

Push all the vegetables up the sides of the wok and add the sauce mixture to the middle. When it's hot, stir in the thickener. Mix well, and mix the sauce and vegetables together. When the sauce thickens, the dish is done. Stir in most of the tamari almonds, if you're using them, and serve at once over rice, garnished with the remaining nuts.

Yield: 6 servings

*Tamari Almonds are whole almonds doused with tamari soy sauce and roasted until crisp. They're delicious, and available in bulk in most natural food stores.

Indonesian Tempeh and Vegetables

The simple ingredients used in its preparation belie the elegance of this dish. It is an authentic Indonesian recipe that is among the most popular I serve.

8 ounces tempeh, thawed

⅓ cup mild oil, such as canola

3½ tablespoons soy sauce

I medium onion

3 cloves sliced garlic

I tablespoon fresh ginger, peeled and chopped finely

2 cups carrot slices (about 2 medium carrots)

2 cups green pepper slices (about I½ medium peppers)

12 to 14 ounces coconut milk (frozen or canned)

Begin by preparing the vegetables so they're ready to add when the tempeh is cooked. Cut the onion into thin half-moons; slice the garlic; chop the ginger; and scrub or peel the carrots and slice them on the diagonal, about ⅛- to ¼-inch thick. Wash, seed, and slice the peppers.

In a heavy, 8-inch skillet, start heating the ⅓ cup oil over medium heat.

Cut the tempeh in half across the width. Stand the two pieces on their cut edges, and use a sharp knife to cut each piece into two thin sheets. Cut each sheet into 8 small rectangles (you'll have 32).

Fry the tempeh when the oil is hot enough to make it sizzle enthusiastically. Cook about 5 minutes, turning once, until it's golden brown, then drain off the excess oil and reserve it. Drizzle the fried tempeh with the soy sauce and continue cooking it briefly until the soy sauce evaporates. Remove the tempeh from the skillet.

Wipe the skillet clean and add 1 tablespoon of the reserved oil; heat it. Fry the onion, garlic, and ginger 5 minutes, then add the carrots. Sauté 3 minutes, covered, then add the peppers. Sauté 3 to 5 minutes, covered, until carrots and peppers are barely tender, then return the tempeh to the pan and heat it through. When the tempeh is hot, add the coconut milk. Stir over medium heat until the coconut milk bubbles gently and all is hot. Serve over fresh rice.

Yield: 4 servings

Tempeh with Zucchini, Peppers, and Peanut Sauce

Cooked this way, tempeh is succulent and flavorful. The vegetables add lightness; the Peanut Sauce, richness. It's a memorable combination.

For the Peanut Sauce:

6 tablespoons peanut butter
1½ tablespoons soy sauce
1½ tablespoons rice vinegar
1½ tablespoons honey
1 large clove pressed garlic
¾ cup water
¼ teaspoon salt (scant)
¼ teaspoon minced hot chile
  pepper (or more, to taste)

For the Rest:

⅓ cup mild oil, such as canola
8 ounces tempeh
3½ tablespoons soy sauce
1 onion
1 red pepper
1 green pepper
2 cups zucchini
2 green onions

Blenderize the sauce ingredients until smooth, then simmer in a saucepan until the mixture thickens, 5 to 10 minutes.

Heat the oil over medium heat in a heavy, 8-inch skillet. While the oil heats, cut the tempeh into 32 pieces as in the preceeding recipe. Cut the onion in thin half-moons; sliver the peppers bite-size, and cut the zucchini in a large julienne, with diagonal ends. Clean the green onions, halve them lengthwise if they're large, and chop into l-inch diagonals.

Fry the tempeh in the hot oil (increase the heat if necessary — the oil should sizzle energetically when a piece of tempeh is added). Cook about 5 minutes, turning once, until it is golden brown. Drain off the excess oil and reserve it. Drizzle the fried tempeh with the soy sauce and continue cooking it briefly until the soy sauce evaporates. Remove from skillet.

Wipe the skillet clean and add 1 tablespoon of the reserved oil; heat it. Fry the onion until it's limp, then add the zucchini and peppers. Cook over medium-high heat until the vegetables are crisp-tender, then add the tempeh and heat it through. Finally, add the sauce and the green onions, reserving a sprinkling of onion greens for garnish. Heat everything through, garnish with the reserved green onions, and serve.

Yield: 4 servings

Braised Tempeh with Cumin-Roasted Potatoes

A combination of cooking techniques (braising, roasting, and broiling) gives this light stew a definitive depth of flavor. The main ingredients are bathed in a chunky basil-tomato sauce. Add to this the mild burst of fire from a single serrano chile and you have, to my taste, a uniquely delicious dish.

For Roasting:

1 pound small potatoes such as Yellow Finn or red

4 small zucchini cut in 1-inch chunks

2 cloves pressed garlic

2 tablespoons extra-virgin olive oil

1 teaspoon whole cumin seed

Salt and pepper

For the Stovetop:

¼ cup mild oil, such as canola

2 bunches fresh spinach (8 cups washed, chopped, and dried)

1 medium onion, cut in half moons

1 serrano chile, or 1½ jalapeños (to taste), minced

2 cloves chopped garlic

½ cup fresh basil, chopped

1 tablespoon paprika

8 ounces tempeh

1 teaspoon salt

1 28-ounce can Italian tomatoes, chopped or squished between fingers, with liquid

1 tablespoon soy sauce

Scrub the potatoes and cut them in halves or quarters to make 1-inch (or larger) chunks. Put them in cold water to cover, set the timer for 15 minutes, and bring to a boil. When boiling, reduce the heat to a simmer. After 15 minutes, the potatoes will be done enough; they'll finish in the oven. Preheat oven to 400 degrees.

While the potatoes simmer, prepare the other vegetables. Cut the tempeh in small rectangles (see page 133).

Toss the drained potatoes with the zucchini, the pressed garlic, olive oil, cumin seed, and a generous sprinkling of salt and pepper in an 8-inch by 12-inch baking dish. Place in the preheated oven to roast 10 minutes and broil 8 to 10 minutes. Set the timer for each function, and remember to keep an eye on the vegetables after the oven is set to broil.

Heat the mild oil in a stew pot or Dutch oven. When it's sizzling hot, add the tempeh and sauté 5 minutes, turning once. Add the onion, chopped garlic, and chopped chile; sauté 5 minutes more, then add the paprika, salt, tomatoes, and soy sauce. When heated through, lay the basil and the spinach atop the other vegetables. Reduce the heat to a simmer and partially cover the pot to steam the spinach.

When the spinach has cooked down, stir it in gently. Mix in the roasted zucchini and potatoes when they are golden brown. Serve the stew over steaming millet.

Yield: 4 servings

. . . .

SUGGESTED MENU
Braised Tempeh with Cumin-Roasted Potatoes
Millet
Mixed Green Salad with Papaya Seed Dressing
Berry Cream Pie

. . . .

For me, a salad bowl is a major purchase, not only because of the expense, but because we use it every day. A salad bowl is more than a mere object; it's an intimate part of our life. The last wooden salad bowl we had broke years ago, and we've been using a glass one ever since. Of course, I prefer a wooden salad bowl, but I hadn't seen the right one. Despite the gorgeous local woods like monkey-pod and koa to choose from, not until yesterday did I see a bowl which totally invited me.

Desserts

Ancient Chinese medicine recognizes five tastes — sour, bitter, sweet, pungent, and salty — and says the ideal diet consists of 20 percent of each. So according to Chinese theory, we crave sweets after a meal because that element was not fulfilled in the meal itself. In other words, Chinese theory legitimizes dessert.

I couldn't agree more heartily. For me, the challenge is to make dessert as nutritionally valuable as it is delicious. With nuts and berries, honeys, syrups, beans (as in cocoa and vanilla), grains, and fruits to choose from, it should be easy as, well . . . pie.

A word here about ingredients. The word is "quality." I'm not opposed to an occasional candy bar, and far be it from me to pass every bakery on the streets of Paris without stopping for at least one pastry. But in everyday life, I want my desserts to add to, not detract from, my overall well-being.

For this reason, I don't use white sugar, which provides calories aplenty and nothing more. Nor do I use white flour, which has been robbed of its nutrients by "refinement." These nutritionally void substances are neither beneficial nor essential to the making of notably outrageous desserts. Perfect desserts require special attention to detail. It's crucial to use the right baking pans, for example. Heavyweight stainless steel is best for cakes. It reflects heat from the cake, so the crusts remain tender. For pies, glass pans are good, as glass transmits the heat directly, making the crust flaky and golden. If you're using a glass pan for cake, reduce the oven temperature by 25 degrees; you may need to bake the cake slightly longer as a result.

Please follow the instructions with particular care and pay close attention to each ingredient. Whole wheat flour is too coarse for cakes, and polenta is no substitute for fine cornmeal. Nowhere are these distinctions more important than in the realm of desserts, where lightness and sweetness go hand in hand.

Carrot Poppyseed Bundt Cake

I've probably baked a hundred of these by now, so many that I don't remember when the idea of combining carrots and poppyseeds came to me. They go together beautifully though, the sweet and the crunchy. This is a moist cake, but I serve it with a sauce anyway; when passion fruits are in season, they make the best sauce, but lemon and orange sauces provide a similar, satisfying tang.

2½ cups whole wheat pastry flour

2 teaspoons aluminum-free baking powder

1½ teaspoons baking soda

1 teaspoon salt

1 teaspoon cinnamon

3 large eggs

¾ cup mild oil, such as canola

1 cup honey

1 teaspoon vanilla extract

¼ cup plain yogurt or soy yogurt

2 tablespoons freshly grated ginger

3 tablespoons poppyseeds

3 cups finely grated carrot

Combine the flour, baking powder, baking soda, salt, and cinnamon.

Separately beat the eggs; then beat in the oil, honey, vanilla, yogurt, and ginger.

Preheat the oven to 350 degrees and butter a 12-cup Bundt pan to excess. Lavish on the butter as if your cake depended upon it. (It does.)

Add liquid to dry ingredients and beat well, then mix in the carrots and poppyseeds thoroughly. Pour the batter into the buttered pan and bake 40 to 45 minutes. At that time, a toothpick inserted in the middle of the cake should come out clean. If you're not positive the cake is cooked through, let it bake the full 45 minutes; the carrots will keep it moist. Cool the cake for 10 minutes in its pan on a rack, then turn it out to cool completely. Serve with Passion Fruit Sauce (page 140).

Yield: 16 servings

Chameleon Cake

I've served this cake dozens of ways, as pineapple upside down cake, strawberry shortcake, custard rum cake, and pecan coffee cake, to name a few. It's a basic yellow cake with a rough texture, almost like cornbread, but tender. Try Chameleon Cake with one of the following sauces and a spot of whipped cream.

1½ cups flour (this may be half rice flour/half barley flour, all whole wheat pastry flour, or equal parts of these 3 flours)

2 teaspoons aluminum-free baking powder

½ teaspoon salt

½ cup honey

½ cup yogurt or soy yogurt

½ cup mild oil, such as canola

2 beaten eggs

Sauce or topping of your choice

Begin by preparing a 7-inch by 11-inch baking dish (a 9-inch square pan will also work). Butter it lavishly. Use too much. This is the secret of cakes that fall effortlessly out of their pans, bringing joy to the hearts of their bakers.

If it's an upside-down cake you fancy, drizzle honey liberally over the butter, then lay your fruit-of-choice atop the honey. Or sprinkle chopped nuts on the honey; that works too.

Preheat oven to 350 degrees.

Combine dry ingredients and mix thoroughly.

Separately, beat the honey, yogurt, oil, and eggs together. Add liquid to dry ingredients and stir well, about 75 strokes.

Pour the batter into the prepared pan. If it's not to be an upside-down cake, you may want to cover the top with berries; sprinkle them on — they'll sink in on their own.

Bake until the cake pulls away from the sides of the pan, is lightly golden, and tests clean with a toothpick. This takes about 25 minutes. But check after 20 minutes; it may be done, especially if you've used a 9-inch pan.

Cool the cake on a rack. For upside-down cakes, invert after 10 minutes. Berry-topped and plain cakes are cooled in the pan, cut in serving pieces, and removed and garnished individually.

Yield: 8 to 9 servings

TRY THESE SAUCES ON CHAMELEON CAKE:

Strawberry Sauce

This sauce is so good and so easy, it pays to keep a pound of frozen berries on hand to make it any time.

I pound frozen unsweetened strawberries, partially thawed
2 tablespoons honey

Blenderize berries with honey for 10 seconds. Pour over cake or ice cream and eat immediately.

Yield: 4 servings (about 2 cups sauce)

Coconut Sauce

Pour this over plain cake, then top with sweet Valencia orange sections, perfectly cleaned. It's also fabulous over the pineapple version of upside-down cake, above.

1¼ cup coconut milk (canned is fine)
Generous pinch of salt
⅓ cup honey
1½ tablespoons kuzu or cornstarch
¼ cup coconut milk

Heat the 1¼ cups coconut milk, salt, and honey. Separately, dissolve the thickener in the ¼ cup coconut milk. When the heated mixture is hot, but not boiling, add the thickener mixture and whisk as it thickens. Cook it about 2 minutes over low heat, whisking constantly.

Yield: 4 servings (about 2 cups sauce)

Passion Fruit Sauce

A single recipe of this sauce provides a nice glaze for the entire cake; if you're feeling more indulgent, double the recipe. No one minds a bit of extra sauce.

⅓ cup passion fruit juice (this is the concentrated juice directly from the fruit, strained of seeds)
⅓ cup honey
I tablespoon lemon juice
⅓ cup water in which I tablespoon cornstarch or kuzu has been dissolved

To make the concentrated passion fruit juice, scoop the pulp from about 6 heavy fruits into a blender; blenderize for 10 seconds (not more or you'll chop the seeds). Strain out the seeds and reserve the juice

Heat the passion fruit juice, honey, and lemon juice in a saucepan. When it's almost boiling, add the water mixture, and stir the sauce until it's thick. Serve hot, warm, or cool.

For Lemon Sauce: Substitute ⅓ cup lemon juice for ⅓ cup passion fruit juice, omit the 1 tablespoon lemon juice, and proceed as above.

For Orange Sauce: Substitute ¼ cup frozen orange juice concentrate for passion fruit juice, increase lemon juice to 2 tablespoons, and proceed as above.

Chocolate-Almond Sauce or Frosting

With no added fat, this cake topping can be eaten with a clear conscience and a totally gratified palate. It's excellent over Chameleon Cake (page 139), with vanilla ice cream.

I cup soymilk or milk

⅓ cup honey

¼ cup almond butter (smooth, not chunky)

I tablespoon unsweetened cocoa powder

3 pinches salt

I½ tablespoons kuzu or I tablespoon cornstarch dissolved in 3 tablespoons cold water

I teaspoon unsweetened cocoa powder (optional)

Place soymilk, honey, almond butter, 1 tablespoon cocoa, and salt in a saucepan and bring to a boil over medium heat, whisking constantly.

Combine thickener and cold water, and add this mixture to the pot when it begins to boil. Whisk until it thickens, then remove from heat and spread while it's still warm on a cooled cake. If a pudding-like skin forms before you spread it, whisk it in thoroughly.

When used as frosting, sprinkle the teaspoon of unsweetened cocoa through a strainer, over frosted cake. The slightly bitter flavor and powdery consistency add an attractive touch.

Yield: enough to sauce a 9-inch cake generously, or to frost an 8-inch by 12-inch sheet cake (about 2 cups)

Cottage Cheese Frosting

When sweetened with honey or maple syrup and blenderized to total smoothness, cottage cheese makes a creamy and delicious low-fat frosting. The trick is patient blending, to erase all traces of curd.

This frosting can be flavored with a dash of vanilla, mint extract, or carob powder.

2 cups small curd cottage cheese

2 to 3 tablespoons honey or maple syrup (or to taste)

Dash of flavoring extract

Place all the ingredients in the blender and begin blending at low speed. Help the blender by stopping and starting, and guiding the mixture into the blades with a rubber spatula. Work your way to a higher speed, and keep working at it until the frosting is sweet, smooth, and creamy. Add sweetener as desired, but don't thin out the frosting too much.

Store cake frosted with Cottage Cheese Frosting in the refrigerator.

Yield: 2 cups

Fabulous Fudge Cake

If there were a Best-Cake-with-the-Least-Effort contest, this recipe would take first place. The whole thing is whipped up in the blender (even the frosting), so in addition to being fast to make and tasting remarkably decadent, the clean-up is next to nothing. How something this simple can be so rich, moist, and flavorful is one of life's delicious mysteries.

For the Cake:

3 eggs
1 cup honey
1 teaspoon vanilla
¾ cup whole wheat pastry flour
1 tablespoon aluminum-free baking powder
½ cup carob powder
½ cup mild oil, such as canola
½ cup soymilk or milk
½ teaspoon salt
Butter for the pan

For the Frosting:

½ cup soft, pitted dates
½ teaspoon vanilla
2 tablespoons soft butter
6 tablespoons soymilk or milk
2 tablespoons carob powder
¼ teaspoon salt
¼ cup walnuts

Preheat oven to 350 degrees. Place all the cake ingredients in the blender in the order listed. Use the high-speed pulse feature on the blender to get it moving, and once it moves, play the blender switches like a musical instrument, adjusting the speed from low to high, and stopping intermittently to move the batter as necessary with the rubber spatula.

Generously butter an 8-inch square cake pan and pour the batter in, scraping the blender thoroughly to remove every bit. Don't wash the blender yet; you'll be using it for the frosting.

Bake the cake until a toothpick inserted in the middle comes out clean. (This takes 37 minutes in my oven.) The cake puffs up like a soufflé as it bakes, then deflates as it cools. Cool the cake 10 minutes in the pan on a rack, then turn it onto a flat serving platter.

To make the frosting, simply blend all the frosting ingredients except the walnuts. Again, use the pulse feature on the blender, and use your rubber spatula at intervals with the blender motor off. Do this until the frosting is creamy, thick, and absolutely smooth. Spread the frosting over the warm cake, and sprinkle it with walnuts. Serve warm or cool.

Yield: 9 servings

Cinnamon Streusel Coffee Cake

Coffee Cake is one of my mother's specialties. It took years for me to develop this recipe, which recreates the crunch and richness of hers, yet uses all whole ingredients. This cake is good as a dessert, with vanilla ice cream, or as part of a brunch buffet.

For the Streusel:

⅔ cup date sugar

1½ teaspoons cinnamon

⅔ cup chopped walnuts

1½ tablespoons whole wheat pastry flour

1½ tablespoons mild oil, such as canola

For the Cake:

1½ cups whole wheat pastry flour

2 teaspoons aluminum-free baking powder

½ teaspoon salt

⅔ cup honey

⅔ cup yogurt

⅓ cup mild oil, such as canola

2 eggs

Combine streusel ingredients in a small bowl, mixing thoroughly. Generously butter an 8-inch square baking pan. Preheat oven to 350 degrees.

For the cake, combine the flour, baking powder, and salt, and mix well. Separately, beat together the honey, yogurt, oil, and eggs. Add the liquid ingredients to the dry ingredients, and continue to beat for about 3 minutes, until thoroughly mixed.

Pour half the batter into the greased pan. Sprinkle with half the streusel. Pour remaining batter evenly atop, then cover with remaining streusel. Use a butter knife to trace a snake-like pattern through the cake, in both directions. This "marbles" the streusel through the batter.

Bake 35 to 40 minutes, until the cake pulls slightly away from the edges of the pan and tests clean with a toothpick inserted in the center. Cool the cake 10 minutes in the pan on a rack, then remove it from the pan to a serving platter, streusel side up.

Coffee cake is best served warm, 20 to 30 minutes after it's taken from the oven.

Yield: 12 servings

Absolutely Luscious Low-Fat Cake

It's hard to imagine that a delicious cake can be made without adding fat, but here's one I relish. It would be exaggerating to say that this is every bit as good as a butter-rich cake, but it's a fact that it's better than no cake at all.

The ingredients may surprise you. Zucchini? Prunes? Why? Zucchini keeps the cake moist, like carrots do in carrot cake. Their flavor is indistinguishable. Prune purée has been found to be an excellent substitute for butter, margarine, oil, or shortening in baked goods. I first read about this in Eating Well magazine, where I learned that, when used in baked goods, the pectin in prunes helps form pockets around the air molecules, giving cakes and cookies added volume and "lift." In addition, prune purée acts a natural preservative.

Because it's tasty, low in fat, and keeps extremely well, we enjoy snacking on this cake for days.

For the Cake:

- I cup chopped, pitted prunes, packed into measuring cup
- ⅓ cup plus 2 teaspoons freshly boiled water
- 2 cups finely grated zucchini (3 small zucchini)
- ⅔ cup honey
- ⅓ cup soymilk or milk
- I teaspoon lemon juice
- ½ teaspoon almond extract
- 2 eggs, beaten
- 2½ cups whole wheat pastry flour
- I teaspoon baking soda
- ½ teaspoon aluminum-free baking powder
- I teaspoon salt
- ⅓ cup plus 2 teaspoons cocoa powder (unsweetened)

For the frosting:

- I recipe Chocolate-Almond Sauce or Frosting (page 141)

Chop the prunes and place them, with the hot water, in the blender. Purée until smooth. Grate the zucchini.

Preheat oven to 350 degrees, and butter an 8-inch by 12-inch baking pan generously. (If you have a reliable nonstick pan, so much the better.)

Combine the prune purée with the honey, soymilk, lemon, almond extract, and eggs. Beat well. Separately, combine the flour, baking soda, baking powder, salt, and cocoa. It's a good idea to run the baking soda, powder, and cocoa through a strainer on their way into the bowl of dry ingredients. This prevents lumps.

Add the liquid to the dry ingredients and mix thoroughly. Stir in the grated zucchini, and when it's distributed throughout the batter, scrape it into the prepared pan with your trusty rubber spatula. Bake until a toothpick inserted in the center of the cake tests clean (in my oven, 28 minutes). Let the cake cool 10 minutes in the pan on a rack before turning it out on the rack to cool completely. When it's cool, turn it onto a flat serving platter and top with Chocolate-Almond Frosting.

Yield: 12 servings

Fudge Torte

Fudge Torte is dark, rich, and thin — a serious treat for serious chocolate lovers.

For the Torte:

4 ounces semisweet baker's chocolate

2 tablespoons hot coffee or coffee substitute such as Cafix

3 large eggs, separated

½ cup butter, at room temperature

½ cup honey

⅓ cup smooth nut butter (hazelnut or almond, preferably)

½ cup sifted whole wheat pastry flour

For the Glaze:

4 ounces semisweet chocolate

1 tablespoon butter

Melt 4 ounces semisweet chocolate in a double boiler over barely simmering water. When the chocolate is soft, mix in the hot coffee (or coffee substitute).

Preheat the oven to 350 degrees, and butter a 9-inch round cake pan generously. Dust the pan lightly with cocoa powder or a bit of whole wheat pastry flour.

Beat the egg whites until stiff but not dry; reserve. Cream the butter, then cream in the honey. Beat in the nut butter, the egg yolks, the chocolate mixture, and the pastry flour. Fold in the beaten egg whites in 3 increments, just until blended.

Pour the cake batter into the prepared pan and bake 30 minutes, testing after 25. A toothpick will come out clean when the torte is done. Do not overbake.

Cool the torte in its pan on a rack 10 minutes, then turn it out onto a serving platter. Let it cool completely.

To keep the platter clean, you might want to tuck strips of waxed paper around the bottom of the torte to catch any glaze that drips down the side.

Make the glaze by melting chocolate and butter over barely simmering water in the double boiler. Low heat is essential here; it allows the chocolate to melt without "seizing up" (becoming dull and hard instead of shiny and smooth). Spread the warm glaze over the cool torte.

Yield: 10 servings

Date Bars

Sweet, rich, indulgent on their own — and more so if served with a scoop of vanilla ice cream — these are the ultimate date bars; they're light, they don't crumble, and they satisfy for hours.

For the Crust:

½ cup butter, at room temperature
6 tablespoons honey
1½ teaspoons lemon juice
¾ cup shredded coconut (unsweetened)
1½ cups whole wheat pastry flour
¾ teaspoon aluminum-free baking powder
6 tablespoons chopped walnuts
⅛ teaspoon salt

For the Filling:

1 cup chopped dates, well packed
1 cup seedless raisins
1 cup water (approximately)
1 teaspoon cinnamon

Preheat oven to 350 degrees and generously butter an 8-inch square baking pan. (Use butter from the cube that goes into the date bars.) If you are using a glass baking dish, reduce heat by 25 degrees.

Cream the ½ cup butter, stir in the honey until smooth, then add all remaining crust ingredients. The batter will be very stiff. Mix well, and spread ¾ of it into the buttered pan. Dampen fingers with water to distribute the batter into the pan evenly; bake 10 to 12 minutes.

While the crust bakes, chop the dates and place them with the raisins and water (just enough to cover) in a small saucepan over medium heat. Bring the mixture to a boil, then reduce heat and cover, stirring from time to time. The dried fruits will absorb the water and become mushy in about 10 minutes; turn off the heat and stir in the cinnamon.

When the crust is ready (almost firm), remove it from the oven. Spread with date topping, then crumble remaining crust mixture atop. Replace in oven, and bake until golden, 15 minutes. Remove from oven and cool on a rack for 20 minutes, then remove bars to a serving platter.

Yield: 16 servings

A-1 Gingerbread

Gingerbread stands out among baked goods for several reasons. First, its flavor is based on the good, strong taste of blackstrap molasses — one of the richest known sources of dietary iron, and an excellent source of calcium and potassium. Anyone interested in nutrition should be interested in blackstrap; here's one of the rare dishes that requires it.

In addition, gingerbread is easily made without milk or eggs, and this version uses very little fat. Still, it is rich, moist, and delicious. That's why it's called A-1.

¼ cup butter, at room temperature
¼ cup chopped, pitted prunes*
¼ cup boiling water*
⅓ cup blackstrap molasses
⅔ cup honey
I egg's worth of commercial egg-replacer (or I egg)
1½ cups whole wheat pastry flour
I teaspoon aluminum-free baking powder
½ teaspoon baking soda
½ teaspoon salt
¾ teaspoon cinnamon
¾ teaspoon powdered ginger
¾ teaspoon nutmeg
¼ teaspoon ground cloves
½ cup boiling water

Preheat oven to 350 degrees. Butter a 7-inch by 11-inch baking dish thoroughly.

Cream the butter. Blenderize the prunes and boiling water, and cream them into the butter. Whisk in the molasses, the honey, and the egg or egg-replacer. (Egg-replacer is a plant-based, powdered egg substitute. For more information, see Brand Names Section).

Separately, combine the flour, baking powder, soda, salt, and spices. Using a wooden spoon, add dry ingredients to wet mixture in 3 increments, in alteration with the boiling water.

Scrape the batter into the buttered baking dish and bake it 30 minutes, or until the gingerbread pulls away from the sides of the baking dish, springs back when lightly touched, and a toothpick inserted in the middle comes out clean.

Yield: 6 servings

* The combination of blenderized prunes and boiling water is used here instead of another ¼ cup butter. If you prefer, omit the prunes and water, and use a total of ½ cup butter in the recipe.

Raspberry Walnut Bars

I've only tasted one dessert bar even remotely similar to this, an old recipe of my mother's called "Ritz Cracker Pie." In an attempt to capture the flavor of that old favorite, yet eliminate the highly refined ingredients, I came up with this honey and whole wheat version which is rich and moist, yet contains very little fat. You'll find these bars truly unique.

1 cup crisp, fine cracker crumbs (I crush two-thirds of a box of Ak-Mak crackers to make this)

1 cup finely chopped walnuts (the blender's pulse feature works well for chopping nuts finely)

2 teaspoons aluminum-free baking powder

¼ teaspoon salt

1 teaspoon vanilla

3 large egg whites

⅔ cup honey

⅓ to ½ cup raspberry jam (honey-sweetened)

Butter for the baking dish

Whipping cream, ice cream, or other chilled topping of your choice (optional but recommended)

To make cracker crumbs, put crackers in a plastic bag and roll them with a rolling pin. Measure, and place in mixing bowl.

Add chopped walnuts, baking powder, salt, and vanilla to the mixing bowl and toss well.

Butter a 7-inch by 11-inch baking dish thoroughly and preheat oven to 350 degrees.

Beat the egg whites until stiff, not dry, then add the honey in a steady, thin stream, with the beater running. When the honey and egg whites are beaten together, fold them into the dry ingredients. The batter will be very light.

Transfer ⅔ of the mixture into the buttered baking dish. Distribute jam over it by the teaspoon, then use the small spoon to coax the jam to cover the mixture lightly. Top with remaining batter.

Bake 25 minutes, watching carefully. The bars are done when golden, and a toothpick inserted in the center comes out clean. Cool on a rack, then chill before serving. As a dessert, serve with whipped cream or a chilled topping. As a snack, the topping is optional.

Yield: 8 servings

Fruit Bars with Vanilla Glaze

Cranberries, dates, raisins, and a hint of orange make these festive bars taste like a cross between plum pudding and fruitcake. They're rich, moist, and chewy, they ring of the holidays, and there's hardly any fat in them.

For the Fruit Bars:

1 cup whole wheat pastry flour
1 teaspoon baking soda
¼ teaspoon salt
½ teaspoon cinnamon
1 cup raisins
1 cup chopped walnuts
2 teaspoons grated organic orange peel
1 cup chopped cranberries
½ cup chopped dates
1½ cups date sugar
1 tablespoon melted butter
1 teaspoon vanilla extract
¾ cup soymilk or milk
2 tablespoons honey

For the Vanilla Glaze:

¼ cup soymilk or milk
1 tablespoon honey
½ teaspoon vanilla extract
Tiny pinch salt
1 teaspoon cornstarch or 1¼ teaspoons kuzu dissolved in 1 tablespoon soymilk or milk
Whipped or ice cream (optional)

Preheat oven to 325 degrees. In a mixing bowl, combine the flour, soda (sift it first), salt, and cinnamon. Add the raisins, nuts, and orange peel.

Separately, combine the cranberries, dates, date sugar, melted butter, and vanilla. Add this to the dry ingredients, and moisten the batter with the milk and honey. Mix, but don't beat.

Butter a 9-inch square or 7-inch by 11-inch pan, and turn the thick batter into it. Use a rubber spatula to even it out, and bake about 40 minutes, or until the bars spring back lightly to the touch, and a toothpick inserted in the center of the pan comes out clean. Cool on a wire rack while preparing the glaze.

For the glaze, heat the ¼ cup soymilk and the honey in a saucepan. When hot, add the vanilla, salt, and the dissolved thickener. Cook just until it thickens, then drizzle it over the squares. Serve warm or at room temperature, with whipped or ice cream if desired.

Yield: 8 to 10 servings

Carob Brownies

These are so dark, rich, and delicious, even the die-hard chocolate-lovers at our house enjoy them.

For the Brownies:

⅓ cup butter, at room temperature

½ cup honey

2 beaten eggs

I teaspoon vanilla extract

⅓ cup (roasted) carob powder, sifted

½ cup whole wheat pastry flour

I teaspoon aluminum-free baking powder

½ teaspoon salt

3 tablespoons soymilk or milk

½ cup chopped walnuts

For the Frosting:

¼ cup (roasted) carob powder

3 tablespoons honey

I teaspoon vanilla extract

3 tablespoons melted butter

Preheat the oven to 350 degrees. Butter an 8-inch square pan thoroughly, and dust it lightly with flour; shake out the excess.

Cream the butter with a wooden spoon until it is completely smooth. Stir in the honey. Use a whisk or electric mixer to add the beaten eggs and vanilla extract.

Separately, combine the ⅓ cup carob powder, the flour, baking powder, and salt. Add the liquid to the dry ingredients and beat well; beat in the soymilk and when the batter is smooth, stir in the walnuts.

Pour the batter into the prepared pan and bake the brownies 30 minutes, or until they spring back lightly when touched in the middle, and a toothpick inserted in the center comes out clean.

Cool in the pan on a wire rack. Leave the brownies in the pan, and prepare the frosting by combining all the ingredients in the blender. Pulse (start/stop) the blender several times, and when it is stopped, use the rubber spatula to move the frosting into the blades. The butter tends to separate at the beginning, but be patient, and a very smooth frosting will emerge.

Spread the frosting on cooled brownies with the rubber spatula.

Yield: 12 servings

Banana Bread I

Banana Bread is one of the most popular baked items here in Hawaii, where bananas grow abundantly. For years, this was my favorite banana bread; the dates and chopped walnuts make it practically irresistible.

You may wonder why there are two Banana Bread recipes in this book, and why they both call for dates and chopped walnuts. The truth is, I created the second recipe as a less costly version of this one. Take your pick, they're both delicious.

⅔ cup boiling water

I teaspoon baking soda

½ cup pitted dates, finely chopped

¾ cup date sugar

1½ cups whole wheat pastry flour

½ teaspoon aluminum-free baking powder

½ teaspoon salt

3 medium (6-inch) bananas blenderized with 1½ tablespoons water and 3 tablespoons mild oil, such as canola

I beaten egg (or I egg's worth of commercial egg-replacer)

½ teaspoon vanilla

½ cup chopped walnuts

Preheat oven to 350 degrees and generously butter a 4½-inch by 8½-inch bread pan.

Pour the boiling water over the baking soda. Mix well and add the chopped dates. Set aside.

In a large bowl, combine the date sugar, flour, baking powder, and salt. Add the blenderized banana mixture, plus the egg, vanilla, and walnuts to the batter. Add the dates and their liquid. Mix well, and pour into the buttered bread pan.

Bake until a toothpick inserted in the middle of the loaf comes out clean, 45 to 50 minutes. Remove the bread from the pan and cool on a rack before slicing.

Yield: 1 loaf

Banana Bread II

When I think of Banana Bread, I remember the 1989 Maui County Fair, where I was called to judge the bread category. There were more banana breads than any other type, and they varied in appearance from a beaming, golden loaf topped with macadamia nut halves, to a little brown log reminiscent of a soggy Tootsie Roll. We three judges chuckled at that one.

Thirty minutes later, when the chuckling was over and it wore the blue ribbon, I would gladly have given a whole stalk of Bluefields for that soggy roll recipe — the best banana bread I've ever tasted. I never did get a copy, but my own version, below, uses dates and walnuts to recreate the effect.

I cup butter (2 cubes), at room temperature
I cup honey
6 beaten eggs
8 large bananas, very ripe, mashed
2 teaspoons vanilla extract
4 cups whole wheat pastry flour
2 teaspoons baking soda
2 teaspoons salt
⅔ cup milk or soymilk
I cup chopped walnuts
I cup chopped dates

Cream the butter, then cream in the honey. Add the eggs, bananas, and vanilla; beat well.

Preheat oven to 350 degrees and butter three 9-inch by 5-inch bread pans generously. Combine the flour, soda, and salt, and add them to the banana mixture in alternation with the milk. Mix well. Stir in the nuts and dates. Spoon the batter into the breadpans and place them in the preheated oven. They will take about 45 minutes to bake; check them after 40 minutes. A toothpick inserted in the center of the loaf will come out clean when its done. Do not overbake. Cool the loaves 10 minutes in the pans, then turn them out to finish cooling on a rack.

Yield: 3 loaves

The fact is, I don't buy casually. I've learned (from buying too much that I only half-liked, or thought I could use or was on sale) that in the end, the only good deal is buying something I'm wild about. Why bother with anything else? Emily Brontë wrote in Jane Eyre, "Do without, but never skimp." That's how I shop.

The Ultimate Pumpkin Pie

Made with fresh pumpkin, fresh ginger, and freshly ground oats and nuts, this dessert is light-years beyond commercial pumpkin pie. Use hearty pumpkin — Hokkaido or kabocha — or other winter squash like butternut, banana squash or even yams, to make this pie. Do not use Halloween pumpkin, it's far too watery.

For the Crust:

¾ cup ground rolled oats

½ cup plus 2 tablespoons ground nuts (macadamia nuts are fabulous here; toasted almonds are very good, so are walnuts)

½ cup whole wheat pastry flour

¼ cup mild oil, such as canola

1 tablespoon maple syrup

For the Filling:

2 cups steamed pumpkin, scooped from the skin

1½ cups soymilk or whole milk

6 tablespoons honey

2 eggs

2 teaspoons freshly grated ginger (or ⅔ tablespoon dry ginger)

1 teaspoon cinnamon

½ teaspoon nutmeg

½ teaspoon salt

For the Topping:

½ pint whipping cream, vanilla ice cream, or vanilla frozen yogurt (optional)

Preheat oven to 350 degrees. Use a blender to grind oats and nuts to flour, then combine the ground oats, ground nuts and flour in a mixing bowl. Drizzle the oil and maple syrup over the dry ingredients, mix well with clean hands and press evenly into 9-inch pie pan, forming a high, fluted edge. Bake 8 to 10 minutes at 350 degrees.

For the filling, blenderize all ingredients until absolutely smooth, then pour the mixture into the baked pie crust. Bake 60 minutes at 350 degrees. (If the crust browns too much, cover it with a few foil strips, shiny side up, to deflect the heat).

Cool the baked pie on a wire rack and chill thoroughly before serving. Serve with whipped cream, vanilla ice cream, or vanilla frozen yogurt.

Yield: one 9-inch pie (8 slices)

Apple Pie Like No Other

In this unusual recipe the apples are half-cooked before going into the crust. This precooking starts the apples' juices running and results in a particularly moist and succulent pie.

If you like firm chunks of apple in your pie, use Golden Delicious, Rome, or Pippin apples; they hold their shape well. If you prefer a more saucy pie, use Red Delicious or Jonathans.

For the Crust:

1 cup plus 2 tablespoons whole
   wheat pastry flour
¼ teaspoon salt
⅓ cup rolled oats
½ cup cold butter
3 tablespoons cold water

For the Filling:

7 cups peeled, chopped apple (6 to
   9 apples, depending on size)
3 tablespoons lemon juice
½ cup honey
1 teaspoon cinnamon
⅛ teaspoon salt
1½ tablespoons kuzu or 1
   tablespoon cornstarch
   dissolved in ¼ cup water

For the Topping:

¾ cup date sugar
3 tablespoons whole wheat pastry
   flour
3 tablespoons butter
⅓ teaspoon cinnamon
6 tablespoons chopped walnuts

Preheat oven to 350 degrees. For the crust, mix flour, salt, and oats in a bowl, and grate the cold butter on top. Sprinkle on the water with one hand while mixing the crust together gently with the other, and, using your fingers, mix it until you can gather it into a ball. Be gentle with the pastry or it will toughen.

Lay the ball of pastry onto waxed paper and flatten it with your palms into a disc. Cover with another sheet of waxed paper, and roll out ⅛-inch thick, rolling gently from the center outwards, and replacing the waxed paper as necessary to keep it smooth. Remove the top sheet of waxed paper. Lift dough on the bottom sheet of waxed paper and invert it over a 10-inch pie pan. Remove the waxed paper and fit crust to pan, fluting the edge attractively. Bake 8 to 10 minutes, until set.

Into a large cooking pot, measure the lemon juice, honey, cinnamon, and salt. Peel the apples and cut them into ⅓-inch wedges; cut each wedge twice across the width. Measure the apples, then toss them into the large pot and mix well with lemon and honey. When all apples are in the pot, heat it until the liquid boils, then cover and reduce heat. Cook 7 to 10 minutes, covered, or until the apples are half-cooked. Add kuzu or cornstarch mixture and stir until the sauce thickens, which it will do quickly.

Combine the topping ingredients until crumbly.

To assemble the pie, spoon half the filling into the crust, then sprinkle with ⅓ of the topping. Spoon in remainder of apples, then sprinkle with remaining topping. Bake 20 minutes, then cover the pie loosely with foil; bake 15 minutes longer. Cool at least an hour before serving.

Yield: 8 to 10 servings (one 10-inch pie)

Berry Cream Pie

I use frozen (unsweetened) blackberries or blueberries for this pie. They're widely available, reasonably priced, and actually fresher than any "fresh" ones we can buy here in Hawaii.

The richness of this pie comes not from eggs or cream, but from cashew nuts, honey, and soymilk. The effect of soymilk, when combined with honey and vanilla, is surprising. It's not at all beany, but creamy and dessert-like.

There are four parts to this recipe: the crust, the creamy filling, the berry topping, and the cashew sauce. It might sound complicated, but each part is simple on its own, and when you put them together . . . but don't take my word; tasting is believing.

For the Crust:

I cup whole wheat pastry flour
¼ cup ground cashew nuts
Scant ¼ teaspoon salt
Pinch baking soda
¼ teaspoon baking powder
3 tablespoons butter (at room temperature)
I tablespoon mild oil, such as canola
2 teaspoons honey
I tablespoon lemon juice
I to 2 tablespoons ice water

For the Creamy Filling:

1¾ cups soymilk, original flavor (not low-fat)
¼ cup honey
1½ teaspoons agar-agar flakes
4 pinches salt
I tablespoon kuzu or 2 teaspoons cornstarch
2 teaspoons vanilla extract

Preheat oven to 400 degrees for the crust. Combine flour, nuts, salt, baking soda, and baking powder in a mixing bowl. Separately, cream the butter; whisk in the oil and the honey, and whip until light. Use a pastry cutter to cut this mixture into the dry ingredients. When the texture is even, add the lemon juice and enough water to form a ball of the dough. Gently press the dough into a 9-inch pie pan; flute the edge attractively, and poke the pie shell in about 20 places with a fork (this keeps the crust from losing its shape). Bake until set, 8 to 10 minutes.

For the creamy filling, start by reserving 2 tablespoons of cold soymilk in a small bowl. Heat the remaining soymilk, honey, and salt in a saucepan. Sprinkle the agar-agar on top, and boil it gently until the agar dissolves, about 10 minutes. Whisk vigorously at the end to help dissolve the agar. Stir the kuzu or cornstarch into the reserved soymilk, and add this mixture to the saucepan; stir until it thickens, about one minute. Remove from the heat and add the vanilla. Pour this mixture into the piecrust gently. Place it on a wire rack to cool, and when it has cooled partially, put it in the freezer to cool completely.

For the Berry Topping:

1 pound frozen blackberries or blueberries, thawed, with juice

¼ cup honey

⅛ teaspoon salt

3 tablespoons kuzu or 2 tablespoons cornstarch

For the Cashew Lemon Sauce:

¼ cup raw cashew nuts

3 tablespoons water

1½ teaspoons lemon juice

1½ teaspoons honey

For the berry topping, strain the berries from the juice. (It's amazing how they continue to produce juice, so keep the berries in a strainer over a bowl.) Reserve 2 tablespoons of the juice and dissolve the kuzu or cornstarch in it; set aside. Combine the larger portion of juice (at least ½ cup) with the honey and salt, and heat this mixture to a boil. Add the thickener — it will thicken radically — then add the berries. Stir them in well and remove from heat. Take pie from the freezer. The creamy layer will have set; spoon the berries over it gently, allow to cool, then chill.

For the Cashew Lemon Sauce, blenderize all ingredients until absolutely smooth. Refrigerate.

At serving time, neatly spoon sauce around the edge of the chilled pie. Cut into pieces and serve.

Yield: 6 servings (one 9-inch pie)

Coconut Tapioca Pudding

This is without a doubt the simplest dessert recipe on record, and devoured by everyone who tastes it. Its success depends on two things: the quality of coconut milk used, and the availability of especially fine, ripe fruit.

If you are able to find Mendonca's brand frozen coconut milk and a sweet, ripe, pineapple or a couple of sweet mangoes, this is the dessert of the hour — made in minutes.

2½ cups frozen coconut milk, thawed

⅓ cup mild-flavored honey

3 tablespoons "quick cooking" tapioca

Egg-replacer for 1 egg (don't use real egg here)

2 generous pinches salt

3 cups seasonal fruit of your choice, chopped

6 sprigs mint (optional)

Put the coconut milk, honey, tapioca, salt, and egg-replacer in a saucepan and let it stand 5 minutes. While it stands, prepare the fruit as necessary.

Bring the pudding to a boil over medium heat, stirring often. When it comes to a full boil, remove it from the heat. Let it cool 20 minutes, then stir, and spoon the pudding and ½ cup prepared fruit per serving into 6 small bowls or parfait glasses, leaving an attractive sampling of fruit on top. Garnish with a mint leaf, if you like. Serve warm.

Yield: 6 servings

Peanut-Chip Cookies

Cookies aren't made more easily or more quickly than this. In 30 minutes you'll be looking at 3 dozen mouth-watering morsels.

6 tablespoons butter (at room temperature), plus a bit for the cookie sheets

⅔ cup honey

1 cup peanut butter

1 cup whole wheat pastry flour

½ cup plus 2 tablespoons rolled oats

¾ cup coarsely chopped peanuts

½ teaspoon baking powder

½ teaspoon salt

½ teaspoon cinnamon

1 cup carob or chocolate chips

Preheat oven to 350 degrees. Cream the butter in a bowl suitable for mixing the cookie batter. Cream in the honey, then the peanut butter. Add the flour, oats, nuts, baking powder, salt, cinnamon, and chips. Mix thoroughly.

Butter the cookie sheets lightly, then drop tablespoons of batter onto the sheets, smoothing them slightly, but not flattening them.

Bake the cookies for about 12 minutes, until lightly browned. Watch carefully to prevent burning. When done, they'll still be soft and will crumble easily until they cool. Let rest about 5 minutes on the cookie sheet before transferring to a rack to cool thoroughly.

Yield: about 36 cookies

Cashew Chip Meltaways

I have little restraint when it comes to this particular cookie. It's sweet, rich, chewy-crisp — all the things a cookie should be. You'd never suspect there's no butter, oil, or egg in the batter. They taste as sinful as shortbread.

2 cups raw cashew nuts
¼ teaspoon salt
¼ cup wheat germ
¼ cup cornstarch
¾ teaspoon cinnamon
¼ teaspoon allspice
¼ cup whole wheat pastry flour
¾ cup carob (or chocolate) chips
½ cup honey (⅔ cup if a very sweet, crisp cookie is desired)

Put the cashews in the blender one cup at a time and grind them to flour. (A few coarse pieces won't hurt.) Combine cashew flour, salt, wheat germ, cornstarch, cinnamon, allspice, pastry flour, and carob chips. Mix thoroughly.

Add honey and mix, first with a spoon, then with your fingers. Mix until the honey is distributed throughout the batter, and the batter holds together when rolled into 1-inch balls.

Very lightly butter 2 cookie sheets. Preheat oven to 325 degrees. Form 1-inch balls of the batter and place them on the cookie sheets. (If you've used the lesser amount of honey, the cookies won't spread too much, but with the greater amount of honey they'll spread considerably, so leave ample space.) Don't flatten the cookies at all.

Bake 16 to 20 minutes (until golden) at 325 degrees, then remove from the cookie sheet and cool completely on a rack.

Yield: about 30 cookies

Raspberry-Hazelnut Shortbread Cookies

These jam-filled cookies are longtime favorites. They're beautiful, delicately flavored, tender, nutty — just basically irresistible. I've experimented with the recipe at length, using different flours, different nuts, different shortenings, and different types of jam. Everything works.

1⅓ cups hazelnuts
I cup rolled oats
I cup whole wheat pastry flour
I teaspoon aluminum-free baking powder
¼ teaspoon salt
½ cup butter, at room temperature
½ cup honey
I teaspoon vanilla extract
½ cup raspberry jam (approximately)

Toast the nuts 8 minutes at 300 degrees, then roll them up in a towel and rub the towel to loosen their skins. Pick out the skinned nuts, and rub those which still have their skins one more time. (If some of the skins stick, never mind; use them as they are.) Put 1 cup of skinned nuts in the blender and grind to flour consistency. Grind the remaining ⅓ cup nuts a bit more coarsely, to a fine chop, and reserve them on a flat plate for dipping.

Now use the blender to grind the rolled oats to flour. Combine the finely ground hazelnuts, ground oats, pastry flour, baking powder, and salt; mix well.

Cream the butter and when it's smooth, cream in the honey and vanilla. Add the dry ingredient mixture and combine well. (The dough will be sticky.) Preheat the oven to 325 degrees.

Form small, walnut-sized balls of the dough, flatten them slightly, and indent the center with your thumb. Be sure to leave a minimum of ¼ inch of dough beneath your thumbprint, so the jam doesn't seep through. Dip in the coarsely chopped nuts. (I form the cookie on the palm of my left hand. The dough is so sticky, I can just turn my hand over to dip the indented side lightly in the chopped nuts on the plate.) Place the cookies on 2 ungreased cookie sheets, leaving room for them to spread. When they've all been formed, spoon about ½ teaspoon of jam into the center of each.

Bake in two batches, 16 to 18 minutes each, until golden. Let the cookies cool 2 minutes on the sheet before removing them to a wire rack. Cool completely before eating.

Yield: about 30 cookies

Carob Chip Cookies

Some people use carob instead of chocolate because the two are similar in taste, and carob has two distinct advantages. It's naturally sweet, rather than bitter (so you don't need as much sweetener with it), and it's low in fat.

But carob isn't velvety smooth like chocolate. Its texture is more gravelly, like a guava, and chocolate-lovers are sensitive to this difference.

So if it's chocolate you love, by all means substitute chocolate for carob chips in this recipe. But if it's cookies you love, try them just as they are.

½ cup butter
½ cup honey
1 teaspoon vanilla extract or
    natural maple flavoring
1⅓ cups whole wheat pastry flour
2 teaspoons aluminum-free baking
    powder
½ cup chopped walnuts
⅓ cup dried, unsweetened coconut
¾ cup carob chips
¼ teaspoon salt

Preheat the oven to 350 degrees. Prepare 2 cookie sheets by greasing them with a bit of butter. Since the cookies contain a fair amount of butter themselves, each sheet only needs a bit.

In a small saucepan, combine butter and honey. Heat gently to melt them together, then remove from the heat; add vanilla.

Mix the remaining ingredients in bowl and blend in the butter mixture. Drop rounded spoonfuls of cookie dough onto prepared sheets, flattening each cookie slightly. Leave room for spreading.

If you bake two sheets at the same time, use two oven racks (this allows adequate air circulation), and rotate the sheets twice, so the cookies on the bottom rack don't burn. Bake 10 to 12 minutes, until the cookies are firm and golden. Place on a wire rack for cooling.

Yield: about 40 cookies

Maple Pecan Cookies

Rich, buttery, and nutty, with subtle maple and oat flavors in the background, these light cookies are good as snacks, and even better as dessert with vanilla ice cream.

1 cup pecans
1¼ cups oats
1 cup whole wheat pastry flour
1 teaspoon aluminum-free baking
   powder
¼ teaspoon salt
½ cup butter
⅓ cup honey
3 tablespoons maple syrup
24 to 30 whole pecans

Use the blender to pulverize the pecans. Blend them until some are flour-like, and some are still chunky. Blenderize the oats until they are like flour.

Combine the blended pecans, blended oats, pastry flour, baking powder, and salt in a mixing bowl. Separately, cream the butter. When it's smooth, cream in the honey and maple syrup.

Add the dry ingredients to the creamed butter mixture; it will be sticky. Preheat the oven to 325 degrees.

Spoon the cookie dough onto two ungreased sheets, forming 12 to 15 cookies per sheet. They double in size, so leave room for spreading. Place a whole pecan atop each cookie.

Bake the cookies one sheet at a time, 16 to 20 minutes. Let them cool several minutes on the cookie sheet before removing to a cooling rack.

Yield: 24 to 30 cookies

Baking Bread

I had been on Maui only a couple of hours when a friend brought me to a remote jungle estate tucked way out behind the pineapple fields. The year was 1970, the pace was slow, and in that sunlit country kitchen a woman stood kneading, elbow-deep in bread dough. I'm not sure whether I even said hello, or just walked right up to her and said "I want to do that." So Jill Engledow, gracious from the beginning, taught me to bake bread.

People think making yeasted breads is more complicated and more time-consuming than it is. They even buy expensive machines to do the fun part. But the joy of baking bread is partly the process itself, at least for me. When, by my hands, the dough rises high, it lifts me up a little, too.

The recipes in this chapter were selected to show how easily and quickly bread can be made. You'll discover that baking bread is not an all-day affair. The secret I wish I'd known from the start is this: The whole process of baking bread is based on flour absorbing liquid; our job is to provide exactly the right amount of flour for the liquid to absorb. You get a feel for it. Read the following notes thoroughly before you begin.

The recipes in this section include yeasted breads and the more expedient "quick" breads, like cornbread and muffins. While yeast breads require at least some rising before they bake, quick breads do all their rising right in the oven. The entire process of mixing and baking a quick bread can take less than half an hour. Quick breads are, in fact, a fairly direct a route to cool, culinary satisfaction. They're a real boon to the spirit, the budget, and the reputation.

Before You Bake Yeasted Breads . . . .

Although each recipe in this book comes with a full set of instructions, it's good to have some background, so you know not only what to do, but why you're doing it, especially when it come to baking yeast breads.

Working and playing with yeast itself is the most interesting part. Yeast is among the simplest of living plant organisms, and its growth is what causes the bread to rise. When the bread goes into a hot oven, the yeast dies and the bread stops rising. But it has already done its work — as it has grown, the yeast has caused the flour in the dough to stretch along with it — and the bread has risen.

So to bake bread, it's helpful to know something about the care and feeding of yeast. It's simple. Yeast feeds on sugar and needs warmth and moisture to grow. Given all three, the yeast (and the baker) are on a roll. To activate the yeast, that is, to rouse it from its dormant state, sprinkle it atop sweetened, warm water. Instantly it recognizes its allies — sugar, warmth, and moisture. Within minutes, the yeasty beasties are stretching and getting ready for work. You can see it happen right before your eyes. Just be sure the water is warm, but not too hot. Intense heat kills yeast.

There are two requirements besides healthy yeast for high-rising bread. The first is wheat flour. Wheat flour contains gluten, the stretchy substance that allows the bread to expand as the yeast grows. If it weren't for gluten, the yeast could turn flip-flops all day, and the dough wouldn't budge. No flour but wheat flour contains enough gluten to give bread a rise, and for this reason, almost all yeast breads with any degree of lightness contain at least some wheat flour.

Once the yeast has become active, begin adding the wheat flour. The goal is to develop the gluten, waking up the stretchy stuff in the flour so it is ready to respond to the yeast. You do this in two ways: by beating the bread batter, and by kneading the dough. I've noticed that if I beat the batter well, I hardly have to knead at all.

You can only beat the bread batter while it's still fluid, that is, before too much flour has been added. Use a wooden, not a metal, spoon, and pay attention to the texture of the batter. You'll know it's ultimately beatable when it's still thin enough to stir easily, but too thick to splash. At this point, I like to give the batter at least one hundred strokes.

Once the batter is beaten, continue adding flour, stirring it in with the wooden spoon. At a certain point it will become too thick to stir; that's when it's time to begin to knead.

The purpose of kneading is to incorporate the requisite amount of flour into the bread dough. What is the requisite amount? It is the amount it takes to make a soft yet not sticky dough.

To knead the bread, turn the lump of dough and all the scraps into a pile on a clean, lightly floured surface. Use a full 2-cup measure to sprinkle out the flour, a little at a time; this way, you'll know the total amount of flour you've used.

Keep the kneading surface and the surface of the bread lightly coated with flour to prevent sticking.

In kneading, the dough is folded upon itself. To begin, lift the part of the dough that is farthest from you and fold it over onto the part which is nearest you. Now place your hands on the just-folded section, and gently but firmly push it down and away from you. It will stick to itself. Now, with both hands, lift the sides of the dough, and turn them in on the center; again, push down and away from yourself. Continue lifting the back of the dough, and pushing it down and away, then the sides of the dough, and pushing down and away, sprinkling flour lightly atop and beneath, to prevent sticking as needed.

The kneading process is rhythmic, and involves the whole body, not just the hands and arms. Use your legs as you push down and away, and notice your breathing, too. I find that I'm usually exhaling as I push, and inhaling as I lift and gather up the dough.

It may take only 5 minutes or up to 20 minutes of kneading; this depends upon the energy and the experience of the kneader. At a certain point, the dough will feel what's commonly called "earlobe consistency." To me, it's "soft as a baby's butt."

Stop at that point — when the dough is still soft, but no longer sticky. If you knead in too much flour, the bread will turn out dry; too little and it will turn out gummy. It doesn't take many bakings to find the perfect amount.

Above, I mentioned that there are two requirements besides yeast for a high-rising bread. The first was wheat flour. The second is time.

It takes time for bread to rise. During its rising time, the yeast grows, the gluten stretches, and the loaf expands. Many bread recipes require two or three risings, but the ones I've developed require only one, two at most. We can get away with fewer risings because one, we beat the batter so thoroughly and two, our loaves are strong, not fragile, because we're using whole grain flours.

After kneading is complete, it's time for the bread to rise. Follow the instructions for rising given in the recipe you're using. Always cover rising breads with a damp cloth, and always be sure they're set in a warm, draft-free spot.

To shape the loaves, use the same motion you used in kneading. Roll the dough upon itself, toward you, with the heels of your hands. Proceed gently, trying not to knock the air out of the bread. The goal is a smooth, rounded loaf with only one seam (on the bottom). Pinch the seam together tightly.

A trick I learned to prevent large holes from forming inside the loaf is to poke the dough with a fork in about 15 places, from the bottom through to the top, right after shaping the loaves. (You can't see the holes when the bread has risen.)

Be sure to butter (not oil) your bread pans well, especially glass pans, which tend to cause sticking. Be sure to put the bread in a thoroughly preheated oven at baking time. And be sure the temperature on the dial has been checked and agrees with an oven thermometer. Also, remember to allow space for air circulation around each loaf. For even color and doneness, rotate the loaves halfway through baking.

When bread is done, it sounds hollow when tapped on the bottom. Larger breads take longer to cook than small ones, and whole grain breads take longer than white ones. If in doubt, give the loaf an extra two minutes.

More Baking Tips Worth Knowing

Gluten Flour is a marvelous product. It's simply gluten, which has been extracted from whole wheat. If you want more rise than you're getting, add a bit of gluten flour. But not too much — about 2 tablespoons per loaf is plenty.

Black baking pans attract heat. Use them when you want a crisp crust.

Stainless steel baking pans reflect heat. Use them when you want a tender crust.

Glass baking pans transmit heat quickly. Reduce oven temperature by 25 degrees when using them.

Remember, it's only yeasted breads that delight in handling. Other baked goods such as piecrusts and muffins want as little mixing and stirring as possible; it toughens them.

Whole Wheat Flour

After reading in the paper last week that 47 percent of Americans didn't know that bread is made of wheat(!), I thought I'd better start at the beginning. Whole wheat flour is ground whole wheatberries.The quality and flavor of the flour you purchase depends first on the quality of the wheatberries themselves. Second, it depends upon the milling, storing, and marketing of the grain.

I couldn't buy whole wheat flour when I lived in Denmark because the Danes mill grains differently. Their coarse milling, which they call "graham flour," is far rougher than our whole wheat, and their fine milling is extremely fine (all the bran is sifted out) and the flour is what we call "white." The situation is similar in America. Different mills produce different grades of flour, and as long as nothing is taken out, they are all called whole wheat. You can be sure that whole wheat flour purchased in a supermarket and organically grown, stoneground whole wheat flour from a natural food store will produce two very different breads.

It's also good to know that when wheatberries are harvested in the spring, the flour is "soft," or pastry flour. When harvested in winter, it's "hard" wheat, or bread flour. They are not interchangeable. So pay attention when you shop for whole wheat flour. Unlike white (refined) flour, it's a live commodity.

Keep whole wheat flour in a cool place so the oils released in milling don't turn rancid, and buy whole wheat flour in small batches for freshness. All whole grains become more perishable when they are milled.

Real Bread Real Fast
For People Who Think They Don't Bake

This quick-rise yeasted bread is the easiest I've ever made. It takes less than 3 hours from start to finish, and much of that time the bread is on its own.

1½ cups hot water

2 tablespoons honey

1½ cups milk or soymilk

2 tablespoons baker's yeast

2 tablespoons each wheat berries and rye berries, soaked overnight and drained (optional)

2 tablespoons gluten flour (find it at your natural food store; don't omit this, as it's responsible for making the bread light)

7 cups whole wheat flour (approximately)

2 teaspoons salt

2 tablespoons mild oil, such as canola

Flour for kneading

Butter for pans

In a large bowl, combine water, honey, and milk or soymilk. The temperature of the mixture should be warm, like a child's bath.

Sprinkle yeast over this mixture and stir once, gently. Wait 5 minutes; the yeast will begin to foam or bubble. When it does, add the gluten flour, 3 cups of the wheat flour, and the soaked berries, if desired (they add good chewy texture to the bread). Beat the batter 100 strokes with a wooden spoon.

Beat in the salt, oil, and 2 more cups flour. Beating thoroughly now develops the gluten in the flour, which makes kneading easy.

Add another 1½ to 2 cups of flour, mixing with a spoon until the dough is too thick to mix. Then turn it onto a clean counter sprinkled lightly with flour.

Knead the dough using the palms, not the fingers, and turning the mass toward yourself in rhythmic quarter turns, adding flour (about ½ cup) as necessary to keep the dough from being sticky. This takes from 10 to 20 minutes.

Butter 2 bread pans generously. Use either 8½-inch by 4-inch, or 9½-inch by 5-inch pans. Add about ¼ cup more flour as you divide the dough and shape the loaves to fit the pans. Use the same kneading motion to do so. Place shaped loaves in pans to rise and cover them with a clean, damp cloth. Let them rise until almost doubled, 30 to 50 minutes, depending on the weather. Preheat the oven to 350 degrees.

When the oven is hot, put the breads in. Bake 40 minutes, then remove the loaves from their pans and cool on a rack. Cool at least 20 minutes before slicing.

Yield: 2 loaves

Cardamom Breakfast Bread

This simple bread requires a minimum of kneading. It is sweet like cinnamon bread, chewy like fruitcake, fragrant like lemon, and rich enough not to need butter. The aftertaste is incomparably cardamom.

⅓ cup butter
⅓ cup honey
I cup milk or soymilk
I tablespoon baker's yeast
¼ cup warm water
I tablespoon lemon extract
2 tablespoons gluten flour
3½ cups whole wheat flour
I teaspoon ground ginger
I teaspoon cardamom
I teaspoon salt
½ cup chopped walnuts
½ cup raisins, soaked 5 minutes in
    hot water; drained
½ cup chopped dates

In a large pot, melt the butter and honey; add the milk or soymilk to the pot. Stir and check the temperature; heat it until it's like a warm bath.

Dissolve the yeast in the ¼ cup warm water, and when the yeast bubbles up, add it to the honey mixture. Stir well, then add the lemon extract, gluten flour, 2 cups of the whole wheat flour, the ginger, cardamom, and salt. Beat 100 strokes.

Add the walnuts, raisins, dates, and 1 cup flour. Mix well. Sprinkle the remaining ½ cup flour on a clean surface, and turn the dough onto it. Gently roll and knead the dough in the flour until it's all absorbed, 3 to 5 minutes. Place the dough in a clean ungreased bowl to rise for 1 hour. Cover with a clean, damp cloth.

Generously butter a 9 by 5-inch bread pan. Shape the dough gently into a loaf, and use a fork to poke the bottom of the loaf in about 15 places. (Poke it all the way through from bottom to top.) This will prevent large air pockets from forming in the bread. Place loaf in buttered pan, cover with a damp cloth, and let rise 55 minutes.

Preheat oven to 350 degrees, and when it's hot, put the bread in. Bake 45 minutes, or until the loaf sounds hollow when tapped on the underside. Cool on a rack for at least an hour before slicing.

This bread keeps well, and makes great toast.

Yield: I large loaf

My new bowl is oval-shaped, and was carved by
hand in Kenya from a wood I've never seen before.
The form is fine and open, the bowl's walls are thick,
but not bulky, and around the base you can see the
mark of the carver's knife. As it absorbs oil, the color
is becoming richer, a mellow golden-green.

What I like best about this bowl is the unusual
combination of clean line and rough handwork. It
was designed by a person with an artist's eye, and
with a feeling for the shape and depth of a vessel that
will hold food. But there is no trace of preoccupation
with detail. It's not the product of a high-tech work-
shop, where half a dozen grades of sandpaper were
needed to smooth the surface. And fortunately, nothing was applied at the end to protect the wood.

European Black Bread

Unlike most breads, which are started from water or milk, these hearty, round loaves are based on beer. This gives them a distinctive, sour taste, which is echoed by a bit of rye flour in the dough. Nonalcoholic beer works fine in the recipe, if you prefer it.

Be sure to open the beer well in advance of breadmaking, so it's flat when you begin. Also, allow plenty of time for these loaves to cool; neither texture nor flavor is fully developed until the heat dies down.

1 cup warm water
2 tablespoons honey
2 tablespoons baker's yeast
12 ounces flat beer
2 teaspoons salt
⅓ cup blackstrap molasses
3 cups whole wheat flour
1 cup wheat germ
2 tablespoons melted butter, cooled
1 cup rye flour
3 more cups whole wheat flour (approximately)
1 tablespoon cornmeal

Combine the water and honey in a large mixing bowl. Sprinkle the yeast on top and wait for it to activate (foam or bubble), about 10 minutes.

Heat the beer until warm, not hot, then add the salt and molasses. It should be warm (bathlike) in temperature. Add the beer mixture to the dissolved yeast, and beat in the 3 cups whole wheat flour, about 100 strokes with a wooden spoon. Beat in the wheat germ and melted butter, then the rye flour. When it's thoroughly mixed, add the remaining whole wheat flour, cup by cup, until the batter is too thick to mix with a spoon.

Dust a clean counter with flour, and turn the dough and all scraps onto it. Sprinkle with flour and begin kneading. Continue adding flour slowly, incorporating a little at a time until the dough has a soft yet not sticky consistency (it takes about 2½ cups of flour to reach this point). Put the dough in a lightly buttered bowl to rise, turning it over so the buttered surface is on top (this keeps the dough from drying out). Cover it with a damp towel and set it in a warm (not hot), draft-free place to rise for 60 minutes.

Butter a cookie sheet generously in 2 spots, each to accommodate an 8-inch round. Sprinkle the round spots with cornmeal. After the first rising, cut the dough in 2, flouring the cut edge lightly, and kneading the loaves gently into flattish round shapes, using a bit of flour to keep it from being sticky. (Before they rise, the loaves should be about 6 inches in diameter.) Handle the dough gently and lightly. Place the shaped loaves on the buttered round spots and cover them with the damp towel again. Let rise 35 minutes, then preheat oven to 350 degrees.

While the oven preheats, use a sharp knife to make ¼-inch deep slashes on the bread tops in a cross-hatch pattern. (This allows steam to escape and prevents cracking.)

When the oven is hot, bake the breads until they sound hollow when tapped on the bottom, about 45 minutes. Remove them from the cookie sheet to a wire rack to cool. Cool thoroughly before slicing.

Yield: 2 round loaves, almost 2 pounds apiece

Garlic Bread Plus

You won't know what hit you when you bite into this delectable garlic bread — it tastes at once buttery, cheesy, and indescribably rich — and it is.

1 baguette (long French bread)
1½ tablespoons butter, at room temperature
2 large cloves pressed garlic
½ cup of your favorite mayonnaise
¼ cup grated mozzarella cheese
⅓ cup Parmesan cheese
1 tablespoon minced fresh herbs (optional)
¼ teaspoon salt (optional)

Preheat the broiler, and set the baking rack about 4 inches beneath the heat source.

Split the bread in half lengthwise. Combine the remaining ingredients and mix them well. Slather the cut surfaces of the bread with the mayonnaise mixture, and place it on a baking tray or cookie sheet in the broiler. Broil until bubbly and lightly browned. Cut into pieces and serve immediately.

Yield: about 10 pieces

Cornbread

For years I called this "Best and Foolproof Cornbread," and it's no exaggeration to say I've served thousands of portions. Cornbread is excellent any time of day, and whether I make it with soup for lunch or with sweet potatoes and black-eyed peas for dinner, it's always my intention to have enough left over to toast for breakfast the next morning. I'd rather have toasted cornbread than pancakes any day.

Because it is made with fine cornmeal and includes both wheat flour and wheat germ, the texture of this cornbread is delicate, even cakelike.

⅓ cup whole wheat flour

⅔ cup fine cornmeal (available in natural food stores)

⅔ cup wheat germ (or corn germ, if you prefer)

I teaspoon aluminum-free baking powder

½ teaspoon baking soda

½ teaspoon salt

I egg

2 tablespoons melted butter

2 teaspoons honey

I cup soymilk that contains I tablespoon lemon juice (or I cup buttermilk)

Butter for the pan

Preheat oven to 400 degrees. Place an 8-inch square pan in the oven to heat.

Combine dry ingredients and mix them well. Separately, beat the egg and beat in the butter, honey, and soymilk or buttermilk.

Add the liquid to the dry ingredients and mix just until everything is moist. Do not beat. Remove the hot pan from the oven and butter it generously. Scrape the batter into the pan, and put it back in the oven. Set the timer for 15 minutes, and stay close to the oven. Watch the cornbread carefully and don't overcook it. The bread is done when it pulls slightly away from the sides of the pan, and when the center springs back lightly when pressed. A toothpick inserted in the center of the bread will come out clean.

Serve cornbread warm, with butter if desired. And bring out the honey once the meal is done.

Yield: 6 servings (12 pieces)

Corn Squares Supreme

I sit here stumped, at a loss for words to describe one of my favorite foods. "Broiled Polenta," the actual name of the dish, doesn't even hint at what it is. These corn squares taste at once savory, mellow, sun-drenched, buttery, and ultimately satisfying. In addition, they're crisp as cracklins.

Although traditionally served with strongly flavored sauces such as tomato and mushroom, my preference is to eat them out of hand rather than on a plate.

7 cups water
1¾ teaspoons salt
2 tablespoons butter
1¾ cups very coarse corn meal (polenta)
3 tablespoons Parmesan cheese (optional)
3 cups fresh, sweet corn, cut from the cob (optional)
Olive oil

Bring the water to a boil in a large pot. Add the salt and butter. Add the polenta slowly, in a steady stream, whisking constantly to prevent lumps from forming. Let it come to a boil again, then reduce the heat to a simmer.

Stir the polenta regularly with a wooden spoon for 10 minutes, then add the Parmesan, if desired. Continue stirring regularly for 25 minutes, until it is thick and no bitter taste remains. Add the corn, stir it well, and turn off the heat.

Butter a 10½ by 15-inch cookie sheet and an 8-inch square pan and scrape the cooked polenta onto them, flattening and evening it out with a rubber spatula. Set the pans on racks (or atop breadpans) so they can cool from beneath as well as above. Let them cool until firm, 40 minutes at least.

40 minutes before serving, preheat the broiler to 450 degrees. Butter an additional cookie sheet or baking tray. Brush the polenta with olive oil, then cut it into squares. I make 15 squares from the cookie sheet and 9 from the square pan. Use all three pans for baking the polenta so there's room to spread out the squares. Broil 10 to 15 minutes per side until crisp: serve them hot.

Yield: 4 to 6 servings (24 squares)

Best Bran Muffins

For years I made puny muffins — the result of following the advice of cookbooks that prudently state "fill muffin cups two-thirds full." But I like my muffins big and moist (and full of raisins) and you must fill the muffin cups to get them that way.

1⅞ cups bran

1⅛ cups whole wheat flour

1 tablespoon aluminum-free baking powder

½ teaspoon salt

1 cup boiling water

1 cup raisins

6 tablespoons mild oil, such as canola

3 eggs, beaten

1 cup soymilk or milk

1½ tablespoons blackstrap molasses

¼ cup honey

Preheat the oven to 400 degrees. Combine bran, flour, baking powder, and salt. Pour the boiling water over the raisins and let them soak no more than 2 minutes; drain thoroughly.

Combine the oil, eggs, soymilk or milk, molasses, and honey.

Add the liquid ingredients and drained raisins to the dry ingredients and mix briefly with a few rapid strokes, just to moisten the dry ingredients. Do not beat the batter, or the muffins will be tough.

Distribute the batter evenly in a nonstick (or well-buttered) 12-hole muffin tin. Or use paper muffin liners. Place the muffins in the preheated oven and bake 18 to 20 minutes, until a toothpick inserted in the center of a muffin comes out clean.

The ticket to perfect muffins is taking them from the oven at exactly the right time. Overcooking ruins them. So stay close to the oven door while they finish up, checking every minute or two until they're done. When they are, let them cool in the tin 5 minutes before removing them to a wire rack. They're best eaten slightly warm.

Yield: 12 muffins

Pineapple Muffins

Fresh ginger, pineapple, currants, and oats combine to make moist, fruity, perfect muffins. When I have macademia nuts on hand, I bake one into the top of each.

1 cup whole wheat pastry flour
½ cup wheat germ
½ cup bran
½ cup rolled oats
1 tablespoon aluminum-free baking powder
½ teaspoon salt
¼ cup mild oil, such as canola
⅓ cup honey
2 eggs
1 tablespoon lemon juice
1 cup minus 1 tablespoon soymilk, milk, or 1 cup buttermilk*
1½ tablespoons peeled, finely grated ginger
¾ cup finely chopped ripe, sweet pineapple, well-drained
⅔ cup currants
12 macademia nuts (optional)

Preheat the oven to 400 degrees. Combine the flour, wheat germ, bran, oats, baking powder, and salt in a mixing bowl.

In a separate bowl, whisk together the oil, honey, eggs, lemon juice, soymilk, and grated ginger. (*If you use buttermilk, omit the lemon juice.)

Add liquid to dry ingredients, stirring only to moisten the batter thoroughly. Fold in the pineapple and currants until blended. Distribute the batter evenly among 12 buttered or paper-lined muffin cups, and top each with a macademia nut, if desired. Place muffins in the center of the preheated oven and bake 15 minutes, or until a toothpick inserted in the center of a muffin comes out clean. Watch them carefully and do not overbake.

Yield: 12 large muffins

Breakfast

Breakfast is the most personal meal of the day. It catches us on the wings of sleep, and brings us back to earth.

Breakfast foods are simple at our house (except on Sundays, sometimes). We've been eating granola with soymilk consistently for about a year now. Before that, it was toast with cheese and avocado, or almond butter and jam. We ate muesli every day for several years, and hot cereal with raisins before that. It's not out of laziness we eat simply in the morning, or even for lack of time. Simple foods seem to work best. I also appreciate not having to think so early.

But brunch . . . that's another story. By ten or eleven o'clock on a slow, Sunday morning, a juicy fruit salad, scrambled tofu, English muffins, and a cinnamon-y coffee cake could sound quite civilized, especially if we've been out walking or in the garden.

Because you can learn to flip an omelette in almost any cookbook, I want to offer some alternatives here. The recipes in this chapter are a sampling of breakfasts that may include, but are not based upon, eggs. We think they're something to crow about regardless.

Scrambled Tofu

Scrambled Tofu is as simple to prepare as scrambled eggs. Make it once from the book, and you'll never need a recipe again. The key ingredients (besides tofu) are curry powder (or turmeric), seasoned salt, soy sauce, and nutritional yeast. Just combine them to taste in a hot skillet with a bit of oil.

Onions and chiles are optional but nice additions, and you can put in other things too, such as scallions, cream cheese, and sweet red peppers. On occasion, with particularly moist tofu, I've had to use a bit of kuzu or cornstarch (dissolved in cold water) to thicken up the juices at the end.

1 tablespoon mild oil, such as canola

⅓ cup chopped onion

2 teaspoons fresh jalapeño chiles, minced (optional)

½ teaspoon curry powder

1½ tablespoons soy sauce

1½ teaspoons seasoned salt

2 tablespoons nutritional yeast

2 cups coarsely mashed tofu (firm or regular, not soft)

Heat the oil in a skillet, and fry the onion and chiles until the onion is transparent. Mix in the curry powder, then the tofu, soy sauce, seasoned salt, and yeast; cook over medium heat until all is hot and well blended. Serve with toast and fruit salad, or see the menu with Tempeh Sausage, next.

Yield: 2 servings

Tempeh Sausage or Burgers

I relished sausage as a child. My family didn't eat it often, so it seemed like a special treat. It was the crispness and the spiciness I enjoyed, and those are the two qualities I set about to reproduce when I put this recipe together.

You can bake or fry these sausages — they'll come out equally crisp. (Baking takes longer, but uses less oil.) The burgers are just as irresistible. Serve them on whole wheat buns with lettuce and tomatoes.

1 8-ounce piece of tempeh, thawed
1½ cups cooked brown rice
3 tablespoons minced onion
1 tablespoon plus 1 teaspoon dark, strong miso such as barley
6 cloves pressed garlic
¾ teaspoon salt
1 teaspoon ground sage
1 teaspoon ground coriander seed
⅓ teaspoon black pepper
Sesame seeds

Steam the tempeh over boiling water for 20 minutes; allow to cool.

Combine all ingredients, using your fingers or a potato masher to break down the tempeh and mix everything thoroughly.

For sausages, form the mixture into about 12 equal patties. They'll measure about 2½ inches across, and ¾ of an inch thick. (For burgers, form about 5 larger patties.) Scatter sesame seeds on a clean plate, and dip the patties into the seeds.

If you're going to bake them, brush the patties with oil on both sides and bake 25 to 30 minutes at 350 degrees (until golden), then turn and bake 15 minutes longer.

To fry, pour a light coating of oil into a skillet and heat. When it's hot, add the sausages (or burgers) and fry for 5 to 8 minutes per side (or until dark, golden brown).

Yield: 12 sausages or about 5 burgers

SUGGESTED MENU
Fruit Salad
Scrambled Tofu
Tempeh Sausages
Ripe Tomatoes
Toast
Chameleon Cake with Blueberry Sauce

177

Pancakes

These are wholesome, whole grain pancakes, yet they're light, as pancakes ought to be. For variety, you can add berries, mashed bananas, or chopped nuts to the batter.

With a nonstick griddle, making pancakes is a pleasure. The Nordicware model we use covers two burners, which means there's space to cook six pancakes at a time. Start the griddle heating on low as soon as you begin preparing the batter, so it's ready to cook when you are.

2 cups whole wheat flour

⅔ cup wheat germ

1 teaspoon salt

2 tablespoons aluminum-free baking powder

4 eggs, beaten

2¾ cups soymilk, milk, or buttermilk

¼ cup honey

6 tablespoons mild oil

Start the griddle heating on low. Stir flour, wheat germ, salt, and baking powder in a large mixing bowl until well blended. Separately, beat together eggs, soymilk, honey, and oil.

Increase griddle heat to medium high.

Add liquid to dry ingredients and beat thoroughly. A whisk works well. If batter seems too thick, add an additional tablespoon of soymilk or oil.

Pour scant quarter-cupfuls onto the hot, lightly greased griddle. When bubbles appear and pop open on the upper surface, flip the pancakes to cook the second side. The second side cooks much more quickly than the first. Pancakes are most tender when cooked just lightly — but on a very hot griddle. It's best to let the griddle regain its heat for a half-minute or so between batches. Serve with pure maple syrup.

Yield: 5 to 6 servings

Granola

At its best, granola is the ultimate cold cereal, full of essential nutrients, high in fiber, delicious, and at the same time low in fat. At its worst, it's no meal at all — just candy in a cereal box. For this reason, granola buyers must be scrupulous label readers. Also for this reason, a granola recipe follows.

Granola is enormously adaptable. Tailor it as you like. The sweetener may be increased or decreased; the oil may be omitted (or butter can be used instead); rolled rye or rolled barley may be substituted for part of the oats; and one sort of nuts, seeds, and dried fruits may be replaced by another. As it is, I find this granola crunchy enough, nutty enough, and almost sweet enough. I add a swizzle of honey to my own breakfast bowl.

⅓ **cup water**
⅓ **cup mild oil, such as canola**
⅓ **cup honey**
8 cups rolled oats
I cup sunflower seeds
I cup mixed raw nuts, chopped
I cup raisins

Preheat the oven to 325 degrees. Combine the water, oil, and honey in a saucepan and heat until they are thoroughly combined.

In a large bowl, combine the oats, seeds, and nuts. Stir in the heated liquid ingredients and mix well. Spread the granola on two large baking trays, and bake about 35 minutes (or until golden) stirring every 10 minutes, and rotating the trays in the oven as necessary for even browning. The exact baking time will depend on the size of your oven and how the granola trays are placed. In a large oven, the trays can be placed side by side, and air will still have room to circulate between and around the pans (air circulation is necessary to prevent burning). In a smaller oven, the trays are placed on separate racks, and staggered for even heat distribution.

Watch the granola carefully so it doesn't burn. It's been known to happen. When it's finished baking, stir the raisins into the hot granola. Let it cool completely, then store in an airtight container.

Yield: I I cups

Mus-ola

This breakfast cereal combines the best features of muesli and granola. From muesli (the nutty Swiss raw oat cereal) it takes hazelnuts and a freshness that comes from having no added fat; from granola comes the warmth and sweetness of toasted grains and honey. The combination is both hearty and light.

Serve Mus-ola with soymilk or milk, grated apple, if they're in season, and honey or rice syrup if you like your cereal sweeter.

8 cups rolled oats
½ to 1 cup coarsely chopped hazelnuts
¼ cup sesame seeds
¼ cup sunflower seeds
½ to 1 cup cashew nuts
¼ teaspoon salt
½ to 1 cup liquid honey (this measurement depends entirely on your sweet tooth)
1½ cups currants

In a large bowl, combine the oats, nuts, seeds, and salt. Add the honey to the mixture slowly, stirring it in gradually and thoroughly. If you use ½ cup, it won't coat every grain, but it doesn't have to. Just mix it in well. Preheat the oven to 325 degrees.

Oil two large baking sheets lightly, and pour the Mus-ola onto them. Place them in the oven on 2 racks, in the position in which they overlap least. What the cereal needs now is careful watching, pan rotation, and regular stirring until it is done. How long it takes depends on your particular oven and the size of your baking pans. In my oven, with two 10-inch by 16-inch pans, it takes 40 minutes. I stir the cereal and rotate the pans every 10 minutes. When done, the cereal turns golden.

Remove the pans from the oven and stir in the currants. Let the cereal cool completely before storing it in a large jar.

Yield: about 12 cups

Hot Cereal

When I cook hot cereal for seminars, it amazes the participants. It seems that most people think they don't like porridge, then find out they do. There is a reason for this.

Good hot cereal doesn't come in an envelope with the instructions "Just add hot water." Good hot cereal requires a certain amount of time and attention on the stove. Given this, it becomes remarkably flavorful, chewy, and nourishing. A simple, steaming bowl of grains cooked to perfection — and topped with your choice of condiments — has an appeal all its own.

Barley-Rye Oatmeal

4 cups water
¾ teaspoon salt (or to taste)
⅓ cup rolled rye
⅓ cup rolled barley
1⅓ cups rolled oats

Bring water and salt to a boil. Add the rye and barley slowly, so the water continues to boil. Reduce heat and simmer, covered, 10 to 15 minutes.

Add the rolled oats, stir, and let the cereal return to a boil. Reduce heat to the lowest possible, cover, and stir frequently until done, about 30 minutes, adding water if desired to thin it. You may need a "flame tamer" (asbestos pad) to prevent scorching if your stove doesn't have an extremely low setting.

Bulgur-Millet Oatmeal

¼ cup millet
4 cups water
¾ teaspoon salt (or to taste)
¼ cup bulgur
1⅓ cups rolled oats

Pan-roast the millet by placing it in a cold toaster oven for 10 minutes at 300 degrees, or cook it on the stovetop in a dry frying pan over medium-low heat. On the stovetop, stir the millet regularly until it is fragrant, about 10 minutes.

Bring water and salt to a boil. Add the millet and bulgur slowly so the water keeps its boil. Reduce heat to a simmer, cover, and cook 5 minutes. Stir in the oats, let cereal return to a boil, then reduce heat, cover, and stir often until done, about 30 minutes, adding water to thin the cereal if desired.

Yield: 4 to 6 servings

Rancheros

If you love a good Mexican breakfast but are cutting back on eggs, here's a tasty alternative that is at once spicy, crisp, and comforting like Huevos Rancheros. The tofu is baked and resembles eggs and takes less than an hour to prepare.

For the Base:

I pound firm tofu
I ½ tablespoons extra-virgin
  olive oil
I ½ tablespoons soy sauce
½ teaspoon seasoned salt
½ teaspoon curry powder
¼ cup (approximately) water
Paprika

And in Addition:

I bag corn chips (5 to 8 ounces)
I recipe Avocado Dip (page 56)
¼ to ½ cup fresh salsa (purchased
  or homemade)
¼ to ½ cup Chinese parsley
  (optional)

Preheat the oven to 375 degrees. Blenderize all the ingredients for the base except the paprika. You may need to cajole the blender a bit by stopping and starting, and using the rubber spatula to clear the blades while the machine is stopped. If absolutely necessary, you can add water, but not more than 2 tablespoons. Blend until smooth.

Oil or butter an 8-inch square baking dish, and spoon the tofu mixture in; level it. Sprinkle with paprika and bake 45 minutes.

While the tofu bakes, make the Avocado Dip.

Warm 4 plates. When the tofu is done, cut it in 4 pieces, and put one in the center of each plate. Top it with Avocado Dip (page 56), Salsa (page 67), and Chinese parsley; surround it with tortilla chips.

Yield: 4 servings

Rellenos Rancheros

Rellenos Rancheros is an egg-free version of Chiles Rellenos. It is similar to the previous recipe, Rancheros, in which tofu is seasoned, blenderized, and baked — and emerges from the oven remarkably egglike.

In this recipe, chile peppers stuffed with cheese (or soy cheese) are set into the tofu mixture. After 45 minutes of baking, the cheese in the chiles is melted and the tofu surrounding the chiles is puffy, firm, and golden. It's fairly amazing that it takes no more than 10 minutes to get this dish into the oven.

Serve Rellenos Rancheros atop or alongside freshly buttered toast, with plenty of salsa (and guacamole, if it's available).

For the Rancheros:

1½ pounds firm tofu, broken in chunks

2 tablespoons plus 1 teaspoon extra-virgin olive oil

2 tablespoons plus 1 teaspoon soy sauce

¾ teaspoon seasoned salt

¾ teaspoon curry powder

6 tablespoons water

Paprika

For the Rellenos:

2 7-ounce cans whole green chiles

6 ounces Monterey Jack cheese (or soy Jack cheese)

For the Garnish:

Salsa

Avocado Dip (page 56), guacamole, or sliced avocado (optional)

Put the tofu, oil, soy sauce, seasoned salt, curry powder, and water in a mixing bowl. Put one-third of the mixture at a time in the blender and blenderize it until absolutely smooth in three batches. Combine the three batches and mix well. Preheat the oven to 400 degrees.

Oil an 8-inch by 12-inch baking pan and put the tofu mixture in it. Smooth the tofu with a rubber spatula; sprinkle it lightly with paprika.

Open the cans of chiles, and cut the cheese into "fingers" to fit inside each chile. Lay the stuffed chiles atop the tofu, spacing them evenly. Place in the hot oven and bake 40 to 45 minutes, until puffy and golden.

These are best eaten fresh and hot. Pass the salsa and avocado at the table.

Yield: 6 servings

So it's sitting
on the counter right
now, absorbing min-
eral oil. And I can
hardly wait to use it.

In Closing

Good Measure

The Problem

By European standards, measurement in America is in its dinosaur stage of evolution. Apparently we find this preferable to the dragon stage, which would mean coping with the "metric monster."

Many people don't realize there's a problem with American measurement. They'll explain an occasional fallen cake with "bad weather" or "I didn't follow the recipe exactly," not realizing that their own measuring devices may be responsible. In the metric system, dry ingredients are measured by the gram and kilogram, while liquid ingredients are measured by the deciliter and liter. A scale or a specially marked plastic cylinder is used for dry measure, while a spouted vessel is used for liquids. There can be no confusion. Here, we use "the standard cup measure" for everything, and the dry/liquid issue is not meaningfully addressed. In order for our system to function without error, which is the point of this whole spiel, we need to use the right cup for the right job.

The Solution

Use a spouted glass or spouted clear plastic cup marked in quarter-cup and third-cup increments for liquid measure. Use flatlipped metal or plastic cups of graduated sizes for dry measure. For small amounts, use a graduated set of the best stainless steel measuring spoons money can buy. They should be deep rather than shallow, and the metal shouldn't bend. Inexpensive measuring spoons (even those made of stainless steel) can be deceptive and inaccurate.

Regarding measuring devices, I enjoy the familiar comfort of my measuring spoons, my nested stainless steel measuring cups, and my beloved four-cup Pyrex glass measure. I'm in no hurry to shift to the metric system despite its efficiency. But when I'm purchasing flour for six loaves of bread, standing in the store measuring what seems to be about twenty-four cups' worth, I realize it would have been a whole lot easier to use measures of weight in the first place.

The Shift

Whether or not America ever shifts to metric, as New Zealand did in one fell swoop, it's good for Americans to familiarize themselves with the system, since it is used practically everywhere on the planet. Arrive in Europe, and you'll measure distance by kilometers, wine by the liter, and cheese by the gram. For comparison's sake, a kilometer is about six-tenths of a mile, a liter is slightly more than a quart, and a kilogram is 2.2 American pounds.

American Abbreviations and Equivalents

tbsp. = tablespoon   tsp. = teaspoon
oz. = ounce   lb. = pound

Liquid Measure Equivalents

dash		less than $\frac{1}{8}$ teaspoon
3 teaspoons		1 tablespoon
2 tablespoons	$\frac{1}{8}$ cup	1 fluid oz.
4 tablespoons	$\frac{1}{4}$ cup	2 fluid oz.
$5\frac{1}{3}$ tablespoons	$\frac{1}{3}$ cup	$2\frac{2}{3}$ fluid oz.
6 tablespoons	$\frac{3}{8}$ cup	3 fluid oz.
8 tablespoons	$\frac{1}{2}$ cup	4 fluid oz.
10 tablespoons	$\frac{5}{8}$ cup	5 fluid oz.
12 tablespoons	$\frac{3}{4}$ cup	6 fluid oz.
14 tablespoons	$\frac{7}{8}$ cup	7 fluid oz.
16 tablespoons	1 cup	8 fluid oz.
2 cups	1 pint	16 fluid oz.
4 cups	1 quart	32 fluid oz.
8 cups	$\frac{1}{2}$ gallon	64 fluid oz.
16 cups	1 gallon	128 fluid oz.
$1\frac{1}{3}$ cups honey	1 lb.	$10\frac{2}{3}$ fluid oz.

Dry Measure

Weight	Approximate uncooked volume	Approximate cooked volume
1 lb. kidney beans	$2\frac{1}{2}$ cups	6 cups
1 lb. navy beans	2 cups	5 cups
4 oz. butter	$\frac{1}{2}$ cup	n/a
1 lb. cheese	4 cups grated	n/a
1 lb. cornmeal	3 cups	15 cups
5 large eggs (2 oz. ea.)	1 cup	n/a
1 lb. dried figs	$2\frac{2}{3}$ cups chopped	n/a
1 lb. whole wheat flour	$3\frac{3}{4}$ to 4 cups	n/a
1 lb. lentils	$2\frac{1}{4}$ cups	5 cups
1 lb. rolled oats	$6\frac{1}{4}$ cups	8 cups
1 lb. potatoes	n/a	$1\frac{3}{4}$ cups mashed
1 lb. raisins	$2\frac{3}{4}$ cups	n/a
1 lb. rice	2 cups	6 cups
1 lb. spaghetti	n/a	$6\frac{1}{2}$ cups

Conversions to Metric

1 oz. (dry measure)	28.35 grams
1 lb. (dry measure)	454 grams
2.2 lb. (dry measure)	1 kilogram
1 cup flour	140 grams
1 cup butter	225 grams
8 fluid oz.	2.4 deciliter
16 fluid oz.	4.7 deciliter

Bean Cooking Time: A general guide for 1 cup soaked beans

Type of Bean	Stovetop Cooking	Pressure Cooking*
Azuki	1½ hours	20 minutes
Black Beans	2 hours	25 minutes
Black-Eyed Peas	¾ to 1 hour	**
Garbanzo Beans	3 hours	30 minutes
Kidney Beans	1¼ to 1½ hours	20 minutes
Lentils (brown)	¾ hour	**
(red)	½ hour	**
Pinto Beans	2½ hours	20 minutes
Soybeans	3 to 4 hours	40 minutes
Split Peas	1½ hours	**
White Beans	2 hours	20 minutes

*The times listed for the pressure cooking are measured from the moment full pressure is reached. It may take 5 or 10 minutes of cooking before this happens.

** Beans with this double asterisk are not suitable for pressure cooking. High pressure may cause them to hiss, spit, and sputter to the point of clogging the vent. Don't try it.

Glossary

Agar-agar is a flavorless and color-less sea vegetable that is used like gelatin. Like gelatin, it must be boiled to dissolve. Sadly, agar-agar is not as reliable as gelatin. As a sole gelling agent it has disappointed me, but it does work well in combination with other thickeners like kuzu and cornstarch.

Agar-agar is available in bars, flakes, and powders. You'd imagine that this variety of forms would add to its ease of use, but instead it has added to the confusion. After years of experimenting with all three forms, I now use only the flakes, and usually in combination with another thickener.

Arame is a mild, pleasant-flavored sea vegetable that looks like black spaghetti. It is very rich in minerals, especially calcium. To use, soak arame 10 minutes in water (it will double in volume). Since arame has a tendency to retain sand in its fronds, swish it vigorously in the soaking water, then lift — rather than strain it — from the water. This method leaves renegade sand grains behind. Cook lightly or use raw.

Arrowroot (see Thickeners)

Balsamic vinegar is rich, mellow, full, and deep-flavored. It is aged slowly in a series of wooden barrels: oak, chestnut, mulberry, and juniper, in that order. The flavor is built slowly, and the result is a magnificent blend that adds character to any dish in which it's used. In Italy, the aging may take 10 years. Balsamic is expensive and worth it.

Beans should be examined before cooking. Most beans are clean and ready to cook, but some are not. You may find broken beans, tiny stones, or little clods of dirt among them. For this reason, it's essential to do a thorough picking-through before soaking and cooking . Use a flat surface like a cookie sheet to make this task easy.

Soaking beans overnight is the gentle way to prepare them for cooking. It gives them time to absorb the water they lost in the drying process and helps them cook faster. When soaking beans overnight, use a large pot (they may double in size); use 3 times as much cold water as beans. Before cooking, drain the beans and cook them in fresh water. (This helps prevent flatulence.) Beans that don't require pre-soaking include black-eyed peas, lentils, and split peas.

If you need to cook beans and didn't soak them, give them an hour's soak in boiling water, then discard the water and cook in fresh water.

Cooking beans is easy if you keep in mind one point — the boiling point. After the beans have reached a boil, reduce the heat so they don't boil wildly and self-destruct. A low simmer will help them remain whole and attractive.

Salt enhances the flavor of beans, but toughens them during cooking. For tender, and tasty beans, add salt and spices *after* the beans are cooked. For bean cooking times, see the chart on page 189.

Black beans, which are also known as "turtle" beans, are dried legumes that are used in Cuban, Brazilian, Russian, and Mexican cooking. They aren't really black, but a beautiful dark indigo. Black beans require soaking overnight and long cooking or pressure cooking. Their mild flavor benefits from assertive influences such as olive oil, garlic, hot peppers, and fresh Chinese parsley. (See Chinese black beans.)

Blackstrap molasses is the first substance that is extracted from sugar cane. It contains a wealth of vitamins and minerals and is rich in iron. The subsequent extractions (Barbados molasses, dark and light brown sugar, and white sugar, respectively) contain fewer and fewer nutrients.

Chinese black beans are soft, salted, and fermented. They are the beans responsible for the remarkable flavor of Chinese black bean sauce, also known as "lobster sauce" (although there's no lobster in it). You'll find them in Oriental markets in transparent plastic bags labeled "salted beans." To use, rinse the beans thoroughly to remove excess salt and other foreign matter. Next, chop them finely. This releases their flavor, but more importantly, it gives you an opportunity to discover any small stones among the beans. I've found many.

Chapatis, or Indian flatbreads, are thin, soft rounds of wheat. They are almost identical to whole wheat tortillas, are inexpensive to buy, and provide a delicious alternative to bread. Serve them warm. Heat single chapatis in a frying pan without oil, or wrap a pile of them tightly in foil and heat in the oven.

Cornstarch (see Thickeners)

Curry powder is a blend of several Indian spices. It usually contains turmeric, which gives it its golden color, as well as cumin, cayenne pepper, coriander seed, mustard, and other spices. The best curries are made with freshly ground spices, or freshly made curry powder. The typical supermarket brands are generally bland; to make your own, see Curried Tofu and Green Beans with Basil, page 120.

Date sugar is dried, pulverized dates. It is crunchy and dark, and less sweet than you might imagine. Be careful when using date sugar as a topping as it burns easily.

Dulse is a strong-flavored, salty sea vegetable. It combines beautifully with potatoes, tofu, and other naturally bland foods. It needs no pre-soaking, but be sure to rinse it thoroughly before serving; small shells hide between the leaves. Its reddish-purple color and spunky flavor go well with salad greens, with red tomatoes, and with orange-fleshed pumpkins. It is the richest of all sea vegetables in iron.

Ginger is a fragrant and pungent rhizome, that can enliven dishes as diverse as soup, pasta, pie, and ice cream. If you haven't tasted ginger ice cream in Chinatown, put it at the top of your wish list.

In the store, look for pieces of ginger that are rock-hard and heavy. Hawaiian ginger, the most common on the American market, is at its peak in January and February, when the color is pale golden and the root is low in fiber. A ceramic grating tool without holes makes a mashy pulp of fresh ginger much as a garlic press squeezes garlic.

Use ginger with stir-fryable foods like green beans, celery, and mushrooms, or finely grated over tender, raw tofu with soy sauce and scallions. Use slivers of young, tender ginger in carrot salad to give it zing — it's not called *Zingiber officinale* for nothing.

Hijiki is the sea vegetable I use most because of its incomparable richness in calcium, its slightly chewy texture, and its clean, marine taste. Soak hijiki 20 to 30 minutes (or until soft) in abundant hot water. Hijiki expands enormously (about 5 times) when soaked, so soak only a fraction of the volume you'll need. As with arame, remember to lift hijiki from its soaking water so any sand lodged in the fronds will remain in the water. Drain and use raw in salads or cook it in stir-fries and casseroles. A sprinkling of soy sauce brings out the best flavor of hijiki.

Kombu (kelp) is a sea vegetable that is widely used in Japanese soups. (It is the base of the well-known Japanese broth, *dashi*.) The fronds of this enormous and fast-growing sea plant contain glutamic acid, a tenderizer and powerful flavor-enhancer. Using kombu in soups, especially bean soups, adds flavor and reduces cooking time. Kombu can also be purchased in a shaker and used like salt.

To use kombu in soup or broth, wipe any salty white residue from the fronds with a damp cloth and place a 6-inch strip of the wide leaf in a small pot of water. Bring to a boil, then reduce heat and simmer 15 minutes. (The leaf may be dried, and re-used.) This quick cooking releases the glutamic acid, but not the stronger-tasting mineral salts, which are broken down by long cooking; if you enjoy a stronger flavor, let the kombu continue to simmer. Eventually, it will completely dissolve.

Kuzu (see Thickeners)

Miso is a strong, salty, fermented paste made of soybeans (and sometimes grains). It is used as a base for soups and sauces. In addition to its unique flavor, miso is also a powerful systemic detoxifier.

In the natural foods store, you'll find miso in two forms. Traditional miso is packaged in squeezable, sealed bags, and is available in half a dozen flavors, based on the ingredients used in its making. This is the product to use for a soup base.

Milder miso is packaged in plastic tubs, and is clearly labeled "Mellow Miso." These mellow misos are well-suited for use in sauces, salad dressings, and dips.

Nori is the mildly-flavored sea vegetable used to wrap Japanese sushi rolls. It is dried in thin sheets cut 10 inches square. The sheets are clean, ready to use from the package. Toast nori briefly over intense heat to make it crisp. As you do, it will turn from purple to green. Wrap toasted nori around anything from brown rice to shredded lettuce. I wrap nori around lettuce, sprouts, and avocado and eat it just like a burrito. Nori very is high in protein and vitamins C, B-1, and A.

Olive oil is a Mediterranean staple that is finally gaining favor in America. Formerly, Americans preferred refined, flavorless oils, but this is changing.

Remember that European olive oil must be labeled "cold-pressed extra-virgin" to insure prime quality. American olive oil is graded differently; any American olive oil that is labeled "virgin" or "extra-virgin" is by definition cold-pressed, and fine quality is assured.

Keep olive oil in a cool, dark place (not the refrigerator; it solidifies), stored in the original tin or in a stainless steel or glass cruet.

Oils To keep life simple, I use as few types of oil as possible. They include extra-virgin olive oil, for its fabulous flavor; pure olive oil, for sautéing where a mild flavor is desired; canola oil for sautés, salad dressings, and baking where a flavorless oil is preferred; unrefined corn oil, for its buttery flavor in cooking and on popcorn; and toasted sesame oil, for its Asian taste.

The less an oil has been treated or refined the more nutrients it retains. The finest oils are **cold-pressed** and **expeller-pressed,** in that order. Store all oil (except olive oil) in the refrigerator to preserve nutrients and protect the oil from rancidity.

Pasta from Italy and the Orient is made of durum wheat. Durum wheat is different than the wheat bread is made from. Coarsely ground durum wheat is called semolina, or couscous, and finely ground durum wheat is used strictly for making pasta.

Durum wheat pasta has become the standard throughout the world because of its mild flavor, which makes it perfect for receiving sauces, and because the texture is ideal — soft, yet firm enough to bite with satisfaction. While testing recipes, I tried every other pasta on the market. I found that durum is the only one I like as well as soba, or buckwheat noodles. These take slightly longer to cook than wheat noodles (and cost more) but they're chewy and delicious.

Why have I tried alternate pastas? Because traditional pasta is made of **refined** flour. Since I'd rather eat unrefined grains, I've searched for a satisfying whole grain pasta. Whole durum wheat pasta is quite good, but it is not easy to find. It is *not* the same as "whole wheat pasta." Eating whole wheat pasta is like eating cardboard. (I suspect it's made with bread flour.) But if you see the word "durum," as in "whole **durum** wheat pasta," you can buy it with confidence.

Another option for upgrading the quality of pasta we eat is to buy "substitute" pastas. They are called "substitute," because they are not made entirely of durum wheat. American law forbids pasta to be labeled as such unless it is made wholly of durum wheat.

Substitute pastas include products like "Slimetti," a two-foot long spaghetti which is based on durum wheat, and has sesame, soya, wheat germ, oats, and brewer's yeast added. Although it is based on refined wheat, its protein content is 25% higher than regular spaghetti and it's delicious. See also pasta in the Brand Names Section.

Pumpkin Halloween pumpkins are bred for shape and size. They were never intended for eating; they are far too watery. But the edible pumpkin, which may be called "Hokkaido," or "New Zealand," or simply "pumpkin squash," is creamy, rich, and sweet. The skin ranges in color from green to orange and the vegetable averages three to five pounds in weight. We eat pumpkin often and use it in soups, stews, risottos, pies, and as a plain steamed vegetable. It stores well for months. If unavailable in your area, use banana squash or butternut.

Red lentils are the quickest-cooking legumes (about 20 minutes) and they make excellent soup. Remember to rinse them repeatedly before cooking (until the water runs clear), or they'll foam up and make a mess when you bring them to a boil.

Rolled oats vary enormously. They range from thick, chewy grains, obviously crushed with a roller, to paper-thin flakes that bear little resemblance to a grain. The length of time needed to cook the oats depends on which type you are using. Obviously, the thicker grains take longer to cook; they are also more substantial and satisfying to eat. A full-service natural foods store has the best selection of (and best prices for) a variety of rolled grains.

Sea vegetables grown in the briny deep are last to be appreciated at the Western table. But sea vegetables have long been enjoyed in other countries, including Japan, Ireland, and the Pacific Islands.

I remember the silence in my eighth-grade science class when the teacher asked, "Does anyone know what we'll be eating 20 years from now?" He answered the question himself, saying "Algae and seaweed, that's what!" "Not me," I said to myself.

Most Americans eat seaweed without knowing it. Sea vegetable extracts are commonly used in food processing — to make ice cream smooth, to create a foamy head on a glass of beer, and to thicken yogurt. And beyond these "hidden" uses, sea vegetables are beginning to be recognized as valuable foods in themselves. (Their mineral content is about fifteen *times* that of land vegetables.) See individual names.

Soba (see Pasta)

Soy sauce, the Orient's most well-known and well-loved seasoning goes by many names: soy sauce, shoyu, and tamari. By any name, the product is a salty, soy-based liquid used both as a condiment and in cooking.

Soy sauce is the general term used to describe liquid sauces based on soybeans. While both shoyu and tamari are in fact soy sauces, they are the elite of the soy sauce family, and can be purchased in natural food stores. In supermarkets, you find two basic types of soy sauce on the shelf. Almost half of the supermarket-type soy sauces are not fermented, but are the result of a one-day chemical process utilizing soy extract, alcohol, sugar, salt, food coloring, and preservatives. The other half are made from chemically processed soy meal that is fermented at an accelerated rate, and usually contain preservatives. These two products account for 99 % of the soy sauces on the market.

Shoyu is traditional Japanese soy sauce, a fermented product consisting half of roasted, cracked wheat, and half of steamed, whole soybeans. This recipe was perfected a couple of centuries ago, when it became Japan's standard formula. Shoyu's depth of flavor is gained by the addition of a mold rich in natural enzymes (Aspergillus), and fermentation for at least eighteen months in

seasoned cedar casks. Traditional shoyu-making is a very exacting and time-consuming process, and the resulting product is deeply flavorful.

Tamari is the liquid that accumulates in the production of miso, during the fermentation process. It has been prepared, used, and sold as a condiment in its own right since the twelfth century. It differs from soy sauce in that it contains no wheat.

If you don't remember these exacting definitions, just read the label on any jar of soy sauce. The best ones say only "water, whole soy beans, wheat, and salt."

Tahini is the Middle-Eastern name for sesame butter. It can be purchased raw or toasted, and can be made of hulled or unhulled sesame seeds. Hulled seeds make a creamy, smooth tahini; I opt for the unhulled variety, though, which is coarser, because it is so much richer in calcium and other minerals. Stir well before using, and store opened jars in the refrigerator.

Tempeh is a delicious Indonesian food made of soybeans. It is sold in a rectangular slab, 4 inches by 6 inches, and about l inch thick. The color is whitish-tan; white from the beneficial mold that holds the soybeans together, and tan from the soybeans themselves. The taste is mild and mushroomlike; the fragrance is clean and inviting.

Tempeh provides complete protein. It's low in fat, free of cholesterol, and is the world's richest vegetarian source of vitamin B-12. It's also a good source of other B vitamins and iron, magnesium, potassium, zinc, and manganese. Tempeh is highly digestible due to the mold used in its making.

How to Cook Tempeh

Like all soy-based foods, on its own, tempeh is bland. In its native Indonesia, it is usually fried, which makes it crisp on the outside, juicy on the inside. Fried tempeh is served with peanut or with coconut-based sauces, which make it even tastier. I've incorporated some of these traditional techniques and ingredients in my recipes.

Tempeh may also be baked, steamed, braised, broiled, and sautéed with success. Since it isn't fully cooked when purchased, it's essential to cook it for 20 minutes by one process or another to ensure digestibility. And for the sake of good taste, it's equally important to season the tempeh with care. A simple dressing of soy sauce, garlic, and ginger works wonders.

Thickeners for sauces and puddings are most commonly, flour, arrowroot, cornstarch, and kuzu. Flour-based sauces are opaque and gravylike, while arrowroot, cornstarch, and kuzu produce a lighter, clearer result. In this book, only flour, cornstarch, and kuzu are used. The thickening power of arrowroot is unacceptably short-lived.

Flour-thickened sauces depend on the union of flour and fat for their good taste and texture. Either whole wheat flour or whole wheat pastry flour can be used. To make a typical flour-thickened sauce, melt 2 tablespoons of butter (or oil) and whisk in 2 tablespoons of flour over low heat; whisk continually until the flour is fragrant and toasty. This is very important, or the sauce will taste unpleasantly of raw flour. Then add 1 cup (or more) of liquid very gradually, and continue to whisk until the sauce is done.

Kuzu-thickened sauces have an incomparably smooth texture and are simple to prepare. Fruits, vegetables, and noodles wear these silken sauces like a sarong. Kuzu is my first choice for thickening sweet dessert sauces, Oriental sauces, and puddings. Unfortunately, kuzu is expensive. Cornstarch, which makes a similar sauce, is slightly more concentrated and much more reasonably priced.

To thicken a sauce with kuzu or cornstarch, first dissolve 2 to 3 teaspoons of thickener in a small amount of cold water. Heat 1 cup of liquid in a saucepan and then add the thickener-mixture when the liquid simmers. Cook only until the sauce thickens and clears, about 1 minute. Overcooking causes these colloidal-type sauces to break down.

It's also possible to thicken sauces with various nut and seed butters. Use ½ cup almond or sesame butter, 2 cups of water, and seasonings of your choice. Blenderize the mixture, then simmer it for 10 minutes.

Toasted sesame oil, also known as aromatic, or dark sesame oil, has a unique, pervasive flavor and fragrance. It's a common ingredient in Asian cooking, and is available in small bottles both at natural food stores and Asian markets.

Tofu is the soy counterpart to cottage cheese. As cottage cheese is made from dairy milk (by curdling it, then straining the curds from the whey), so tofu is made from soy milk. Only in the case of tofu, the curds are larger and bond more easily, so it is formed into "cakes" or "blocks," while dairy curds are seasoned with salt and cream, and sold in cartons.

As Westerners, we expect our food, especially our protein food, to be strong-flavored and chewy, like meat. Many people think they don't like tofu because it hasn't been prepared to taste that way. But it's possible to transform tofu from the original, square bland block into a most appealing dish. I wish I had a mango for every person who's told me they never liked tofu until they tried it in my curry, my Parmesan, or with my Black Bean Sauce.

There's no secret to making tofu appealing to the Western palate, it's just a matter of marinating it in soy sauce for a short while, and placing it on a hot griddle or frying pan. This small procedure makes a phenomenal difference. In fact, if I could tell you only one thing about tofu, it would be: Try this. Buy a pound of firm tofu, slice it in half-inch slabs, marinate it for about 10 minutes in soy sauce, then cook it on a hot, non-stick pan until it becomes crusty and golden, about 10 minutes per side. Then taste it.

When you see fresh tofu in the store, it is usually packed in plastic tubs in water. This type of tofu has an expiration date, and must be kept in the refrigerator. Once opened, you can

extend the life of the unused portion by changing the water daily, for about a week.

Somewhere on the package of tofu you'll see the label **soft** or **firm.** (On Maui, we also have "regular" tofu, which is in between. It is my tofu of choice, with the firm type running second.) Firm tofu is easy to slice or cube and, once marinated and grilled, holds its shape well in stir-fries, stews, and casseroles.

You can also buy tofu in aseptic cartons. This tofu doesn't require refrigeration until it is opened. While less fresh, this product has two very appealing features. First, convenience. Boxed tofu is wonderful to take camping, and to keep in the cupboard as a back-up supply. It also has a particularly smooth consistency and is unbeatable for making preparations such as tofu mayonnaise, which require a smooth product. Because of its texture, this tofu is labelled **silken.** (For more information, see Brand Names Section.)

Ume plum vinegar is among my favorite condiments. Its color is a clear, deep pink, its flavor at once sour and salty, but not sharp. We use it in combination with extra-virgin olive oil over plain pasta; I never tire of the clean, crisp taste. Ume plum is the only vinegar listed here which must be purchased in a natural foods store.

Vinegar is acidic by nature. It ranges from 4% to 7½% acidity, and within those few percentage points there is room for enormous variation in strength, sourness, and fullness of taste. Combine different vinegars to make interesting, unique salad dressings. I love balsamic , rice vinegar, ume plum vinegar, and red and white wine vinegars.

Wakame is a cousin to the sea vegetable kombu and is also effective as a tenderizer. Wakame itself is far more tender than kombu, though. Soak it briefly to ready wakame for use. If it has a thick mid-rib, cut it out with a pair of scissors; add the delicate leaves to soups or salads. Wakame is delicious when served as a condiment sprinkled with soy sauce and toasted sesame seeds.

Brand Names Section

Quality food products aren't created by chance, they are created by people who value high-quality foods. These are the people I like to support, and I'm happy to route my food dollars their way.

Aluminum-free baking powder: Rumford's Baking Powder has been on the market for decades, and is still the best. It contains no aluminum and leaves no metallic residue in your baked goods.

Baker's yeast: I use Saf-Instant, which contributes to a fast-rising bread. It is available in 1 pound packages and will last almost indefinitely when stored in a cool place.

Bouillon cubes: Hugli, a Swiss brand, has good flavor and is reasonably priced. The recipes in this book were tested with Hugli regular cubes, which contain salt. Each cube flavors 2¼ cups of water.

Coconut milk: Mendonca's frozen product is pure, and a pure delight. It is preferable to canned coconut milk, which has been cooked, and which usually contains preservatives.

Dairy products: It is particularly important to buy dairy products from a company you trust. I buy Alta Dena brand butter and cheeses.

Egg-replacer: Ener-G brand egg-replacer does the best job of any commercial product I've tried. It reproduces the binding power of eggs in baked goods and casseroles, but it's not a substitute for omelettes or soufflés. In truth, nothing binds exactly like eggs, but when you need or want to reduce your total egg intake, this product can help.

Enchilada sauce: Las Palmas brand is authentic. It's based on chiles, rather than tomatoes, and it contains no lard.

Firm, silken tofu: Mori-Nu packages tofu in a revolutionary, 10.5 ounce aseptic carton that needs no refrigeration until it is opened. Not only is this the longest-lasting tofu available, it's the smoothest. Keep some on hand for quick and easy dressings and sauces.

Grain beverage: Cafix is the grain beverage I prefer when I want something heartier than tea and less stimulating than coffee.

Green chiles (whole or chopped): Ortega brand chiles are consistently good and widely available. I use their whole chiles, diced chiles, and green-chile salsa.

Mirin: This Japanese seasoning, produced by Eden brand, is made of rice, well water, and sea salt; its sweetness comes from the rice. Use mirin in dressings and sauces for subtle sweetness.

Nutritional yeast: Red Star brand makes a delicious, flaked product, which is available in bulk in natural food stores. Kal is another good brand. (It is prepackaged.)

Oils: Fortuna brand is my choice for extra-virgin olive oil, for its fine flavor and reasonable price. Hain is the brand I prefer for mild oils, such as canola, and Spectrum brand produces a wonderful, buttery, unrefined corn oil.

Pasta: De Cecco makes great pasta; so do De Boles and Eden. They're relatively expensive, though, if you (like me) think pasta is supposed to be economical. The best pasta value is a spaghetti called Slimetti, which is available in natural food stores. (I wish they made other shapes too.)

Ramen soup mix: Westbrae makes this squiggly noodle soup mix in a variety of flavors.

Seasoned salt: Spike brand is available in natural food stores. I order two additional seasoned salt mixtures (Greek and Italian style) from San Francisco Herb Company, 250 14th St., San Francisco, CA 94103.

Soba noodles: Also known as buckwheat noodles, soba is tan in color and slightly coarser in texture than pasta made of wheat. It is only made in one shape, similar to spaghetti. My favorite brands are Shirakiku (Shinsu soba) and Mum's (Kumamoto soba). These products are available in Oriental markets, where they are far less expensive than the macrobiotic brands found in natural food stores.

Soymilk: There are many good brands of soymilk on the market; I use Edensoy (original flavor). You can purchase carob, vanilla, and other flavors of soymilk, which are fine for drinking, but are not suitable for cooking.

It's important to remember that soymilk is not intended to replace dairy milk; it has far less calcium. (It's also true that the value of dairy milk as a source of calcium is being reevaluated at present.) It is, however, an excellent source of protein, and it works well as a replacement for dairy milk in most recipes.

Tahini: Westbrae makes good tahini, as does Maranatha. I prefer the product called Sesame Butter, which is made with unhulled seeds.

Tempeh and tempeh cutlets: White Wave brand makes 8-ounce slabs of tempeh from various bean-grain mixtures. (I prefer the plain soy variety.) Find tempeh in the frozen foods section of natural food stores.

Ume plum vinegar: Eden foods is responsible for the production of this most remarkable product. It's available in natural food stores.

Index